No Principal Left Behind:

Leadership Coaching for the 21st Century

Fannie Lovelady-Spain, Ph.D.

With Melody Dawson, PMP

Lovelady School Leadership Press

Copyright © 2011 by Lovelady School Leadership Press
Reprinted 2012

Materials appearing here are copyrighted. With one exception, all rights are reserved. Readers may reproduce only those pages marked "Reproducible." Otherwise, no part of this book may be reproduced or transmitted in any form or by any means (electronic, photocopying, recording, or otherwise) without prior written permission of the publisher and the author.

Every effort has been made to trace and acknowledge copyright materials. Should any infringements have occurred accidentally, the authors and publishers tender their apologies.

Notice of Liability: The information in this book is distributed on an "as is" basis, without warranty. While every precaution has been taken in the preparation of the book, neither the authors nor Lovelady School Leadership Consulting, LLC shall have any liability to any person or entity with respect to any loss or damage caused or alleged to be caused directly or indirectly by the instructions contained in this book.

For more information:
Lovelady School Leadership Press
PO Box 621
Rockdale TX 76567

1-877-368-0004
Email: MyCoach@loveladyschoolleadershp.com
www.LoveLadySchoolLeadership.com

Printed in the United States of America

Library of Congress Control Number: 2011918717
Lovelady-Spain, Fannie L.
No Principal Left Behind: Leadership Coaching for the 21st Century and Beyond/ Fannie Lovelady-Spain, Melody Dawson.

Includes bibliographical references

Book Interior Design: www.KarrieRoss.com

ISBN: 978-0-9847313-0-5

1.Leadership Coaching 2. School Principal 3. Staff Development 4. Educational Leadership 5. Professional Development
I. Title

Visit MyCoach Interactive™ at
www.LoveladySchoolLeadership.com
to download reproducibles in this book.

DEDICATION

This book is dedicated with all my love to my grandson, Dawson Fortes Dos Santos, who will be entrusted to carry the Lovelady legacy into the future, and my daughter Melody Dawson, whose love is a force that wills me to give my best to the world.

This book is also dedicated in memory of my mother, Fannie Lovelady, whose vision and love for me are still propelling my life; my father, Artis Lovelady, whose "jewels in the junkyard" still thrive; and my sisters and brothers who have passed on – Dr. Uline Hughes, Dr. Hubert Glen Lovelady, Dr. Artis Ruth Hopkins, and Hulen Dean Lovelady – from whom I inherited the best of my character.

Finally, to my brothers Willie Henry Lovelady and Brent Sherrill Lovelady, who enrich my life to this day.

ACKNOWLEDGMENTS

Special thanks go to my daughter, Melody Dawson, whose vision and belief in me never wavers. Special thanks go to Luis for making sure we were nourished with delicious Cape Verdean meals during the many months spent writing this book. I especially thank Elbert for generously offering an established platform in which to present our ideas and to Bill for consulting assistance. Thanks to Marjorie, my former secretary, for her support, loyalty, and for the cheerful messages that keep coming. For my dear friends, Marion and Bob, for the friendship they have given me for many years; I cherish you both. My deep affection for Elvira and Felix for their friendship and support; you will always have a special place in my heart. Thanks to Monty, Treva, Pat, and Elaine for their well wishes and constant support. For my friend Bart, you can never know the profound spiritual lessons you taught me that still guide my life. I am indebted to the many students, teachers, and staff with whom I worked, and the many parents who entrusted their children's school lives into my care. I am grateful to the mentors, many of whom have passed on, for allowing me to choose them and learn from them while I sought to become a better administrator.

Melody and I give special thanks to the superintendent, the assistant superintendent and the principals of the Rockdale Independent School District in Rockdale, Texas, for being our Focus Group to test and critique our ideas and materials. We also thank the following for playing key roles in the making of this book:

Karrie Ross	Be It Now! Design, for her seamless book publishing and interior layout design expertise
Jenny Meadows	My Copy Editor, for expert editing
Nicole Weil Simonich	Horizon Film and Video, for extraordinary media direction and production
Paul Murski	Horizon Film and Video, for outstanding editing and camera work
Jennifer Alt	Jennifer Alt Design, for flawless final book cover graphic design
Felix Cheung	For graphic designs
Roger Glenn	Mach 1 Media, for the meticulous development that brought this book to life on the website

ABOUT LOVELADY SCHOOL LEADERSHIP CONSULTING

Our Vision:

To change the educational leadership professional development paradigm by providing principals with leadership coaching and a systematic change process to transform their schools and increase student outcomes.

Our Mission:

To incorporate leadership coaching as a standard practice in professional development programs for principals and leadership teams and to establish the School Principal Change Model™ as a process used by principals, leadership teams and parents to improve their schools.

Our Goal:

To develop the knowledge and skills of school principals and leadership teams through effective leadership and change strategies and measurably increase student achievement and transform schools.

ABOUT THE AUTHORS

Fannie Lovelady-Spain, Ph.D

Co-Founder and Expert School Change Coach

Dr. Lovelady-Spain is a former principal with experience leading all K-12 levels. An Expert School Change Coach, she coaches schools to become more effective learning institutions, and she coaches principals into leadership actions directly linked to Assessment, Curriculum, and Instruction. She utilizes the School Principal Change Model™ – a school transformation process she developed that includes the entire school community: principal, parents, students, leadership teams, faculty, and district management. She recently proved the success of the School Principal Change Model™ by leading two previously underachieving Navajo Nation schools to accomplish Adequate Yearly Progress (AYP).

Dr. Lovelady-Spain is a former Administrator and Education Manager; she has been a principal over two decades inside the Bureau of Indian Education, Grant, Public, Charter, Community, Court, and Private Schools in California, Texas, Arizona, and New Mexico.

In 1979, while serving as a Policy Fellow with the Institute for Educational Leadership, The George Washington University, Washington, D.C., Dr. Lovelady-Spain developed the framework for the California School Leadership Academy, a two-part initiative that addressed both research and training. As Manager of the School Leadership Unit for the California Department of Education, she finalized the California School Leadership Academy program that researched and trained school leaders all over the state of California. Today, there are Regional Training Centers throughout the State of California with ongoing Research and Training Development.

As a Policy Fellow with the National Institute of Education (NIE), Dr. Lovelady-Spain traveled extensively to collect field research on the state of training for principals. She visited the Harvard Principals' Center and many local, state, county, university, and school districts. Her research findings led to Request for Proposals (RFP) from well-known researchers and firms throughout the country and resulted in three published articles:

- Dawson, Fannie L. "Women and Minorities in the Principalship: Career Opportunities and Problems." National Association of Secondary Principals, NASSP Bulletin, Vol. 64, No. 440, December 1980.

- Dawson, Fannie L. "No Room at the Top." National Association of Elementary Principals, NAESP Principal Journal, Vol. 61, No. 1, September 1981.

- Shakeshaft, et al. "Strategies for Overcoming the Barriers to Women in School Administration: Achieving Sex Equity through Education." Johns Hopkins Press, Fall 1983.

Dr. Spain received her Bachelor of Music degree from the University of North Texas, Denton, Texas; her Master of Science degree in School Administration from California State University in Hayward; and her Ph.D. in Education Administration from Sierra University in Costa Mesa, California.

As part of her civic duties, Dr. Lovelady-Spain is the Founder of the Fannie Page Lovelady Foundation that sponsors leadership trainings for young students in high school and college. She has been a member of the 10th Texas Silver-Haired Legislature, served one elected term as City Councilwoman for the City of Rockdale in Texas, and served as a member of the Milam County Historical Commission.

Melody Dawson, B.A., PMP

Co-Founder and Chief Operating Officer

As Lovelady School Leadership's chief operating officer, Melody Dawson is responsible for the strategic development and operational leadership of the company's sales, marketing, and services. Globally certified and skilled in project management, her areas of expertise lie in quality management, process improvement, and operational infrastructure development.

Ms. Dawson earned a BA in History from the prestigious University of California at Los Angeles. Prior to co-founding the company, Ms. Dawson co-founded and served as chief operating officer for an online start-up. Her professional experience stems from a successful career working in domestic and global business management roles for technology corporations such as Symantec and Dell.

Ms. Dawson currently serves as a City Council Member in Rockdale, Texas. She is an active Rockdale Lions Club member and participates in Leadership Milam, a leadership program comprised of leaders in the county, including elected officials, CEOs, School Superintendants, Chamber of Commerce Presidents, attorneys, and bank presidents.

Ms. Dawson is passionate about education reform and actively serves her community in leadership programs and those that advocate for our nation's youth. She serves on the board of the Rockdale YMCA that functions in conjunction with the Rockdale Municipal Development District. Her long-term strategy of economic development for the Central Texas Region, is to inspire entrepreneurship by establishing Junior Achievement in schools throughout Milam county.

INTRODUCTION

This book is a compilation of my experience as a school principal. I first became interested in the role of the principal after working as a Human Relations Specialist in the Oakland Unified School District, Oakland, California. During the 1960s, there was unrest in the nation on every front. This unrest carried forward to the 1970s, particularly in the Oakland/Berkeley/San Francisco Bay Area. Demonstrations were occurring at the University of California at Berkeley; the Black Panther Movement was in full swing in Oakland; the hippie movement was alive and well in San Francisco; and Vietnam War demonstrations were occurring all over the country. The Symbionese Liberation Army was active and would eventually have a personal impact upon me; specifically, in November of 1973, Dr. Marcus Foster, Superintendent of the Oakland Unified School District, who selected me for my first principal position, was gunned down after leaving a board meeting.

The Human Relations Division of the Oakland Unified Schools was created to offer guidance and trainings that would bring the communities together in the midst of the unrest happening around the schools. We designed diversity trainings to engage educators and communities in dialogue about our similarities, differences and unique contributions to society. My particular assignment included one high school and all of its feeder junior and elementary schools. I was responsible for working with the schools to recruit parents and community members to participate in the decision-making process at all of the schools.

I became very aware of the many challenges that principals faced during these turbulent years. I gained a great respect for the courage and dedication of those principals in particular, and all educators in general as they continued to educate the young people. The students were beset by so many distractions, but the schools continued to offer them opportunities to succeed.

I was also profoundly impacted by a life-threatening incident that occurred in my school during my first year as a principal. During the occurrence, I intuitively made the right decisions and kept myself and my entire staff safe; however, I am certain that if I had been given the benefit of dialogue, reflection and feedback about various situations that I would encounter as a principal, I would have felt more secure in my decision-making going forward. I found myself isolated and overwhelmed with the enormity of the responsibilities.

As a result of the experience, my insight into principal preparation and ongoing professional development was forever changed. I vowed right then that my mission would be to research and test effective strategies, document the results, and someday be able to confidently lobby for more effective leadership development for principals and those aspiring to be school leaders.

That 'someday' is now. This book calls for a new paradigm in the preparation and ongoing trainings for principals. Studies show that the principal is the most effective agent for bringing about educational improvement, and ongoing staff development is critical to effective school leadership. However, most staff development for principals is not aligned with instructional leadership, and workshops are uncoordinated and fragmented. According to many principals I have spoken with over the years, their academic and managerial trainings did not provide them with instructional leadership skills, nor were they made aware of the many mandates heaped on them by the federal, state, courts and by school boards, many of which have little to no effect on teaching and learning.

I had dual purposes for writing this book. First, to recommend *onsite, site-specific and ongoing* leadership coaching to principals, designed to support their growth in personal and leadership competencies; and second, to introduce a field-tested, research-based continuous improvement process, the School Principal Change Model™, which can be used by principals and school teams to transform their schools.

Chapters 4 and 5 of this book can be used as a self-study text. They provide an in-depth understanding of what the change process is and how it works. In Chapter 8, you will encounter 'how to' exercises, activities and presentations. These tools, techniques and other resources are designed to support the implementation of the 5 Phases of the School Principal Change Model™.

Table of Contents

CHAPTER 1

A PRINCIPAL ON PURPOSE – WITH A PURPOSE

Caught in a Campus Crossfire 19
    Motivating Factor 19
    Turmoil in Nation 20
    Fully Confident 21
    The Incident 21
    Police Arrival 23
    Shots Heard 23
    Turn of Events 24
    Hysteria in Gymnasium 24
    The Gravity of the Moment 25
    Rush to Judgment 25
    Standoff and Capture 26
    The Arms of My Sisters 26
    Quick Recovery 27
Surviving Neglect 27
    Pre-Service and In-Service Preparation .27
    Out of Necessity 28
    Becoming My Own Leadership Coach .28
    Documenting the Coaching Process 29
    The Birth of the School Principal Change Model™ 29
    Reading as a Systems Approach 30
    My Appeal to Our Leaders in Education 30

CHAPTER 2

THE 21st CENTURY CHALLENGE

Removing Barriers 33
    A New Call for Leadership 34

Breaking The Cycle 35
What You Need to Know about Change 38
Principal Work Overload 39

CHAPTER 3

WHAT LEAVES PRINCIPALS BEHIND

Changing Tradition - A New Paradigm 45
    Organizational Culture and Tradition 46
    Budget Priorities and Allocations 47
    Leadership Impact on Student Learning 48
    Staff Development Program Design 49

CHAPTER 4

THE SCHOOL PRINCIPAL CHANGE MODEL™

How It Works 55
    Phase 1: Vision 59
    Phase 2: Mission 65
    Phase 3: Plan 70
    Phase 4: Action 73
    Phase 5: Results 80

CHAPTER 5

THE SCHOOL PRINCIPAL CHANGE MODEL™ COMBINED WITH LEADERSHIP COACHING — A REMEDY

A New Approach for the Ongoing Staff Development of Principals 83
    The Right Strategy 84
    Brief History of Coaching 88
    Leadership Coaching Defined: What Coaching Is .88
    What Coaching Is Not 90
    How Coaching Works 92

How Coaching Is Initiated 94
Adult Learning Assumptions in Coaching Process 96

CHAPTER 6

REVIEW OF THE RELEVANT RESEARCH

Best Practices for Effective Leadership and Coaching 99
About Effective Leadership 100
Selected Models and Programs 103

CHAPTER 7

CONCLUSION 111

CHAPTER 8

TOOLS, TECHNIQUES AND OTHER RESOURCES

The Play Book: "You Can Do It!" 115
How to Create a Shared School Vision – Phase 1 117
How to Create a School Mission Statement – Phase 2 134
How to Plan for Action – Phase 3 141
Appendices 146
How to Take Action – Phase 4 156
How to Get Results – Phase 5 165
Other Resources 171
The Principal as Curriculum Leader 171
How to Analyze Data 176
How to Align Your Total Program 178
Aligning Instruction and Observations – Activity Sheets 180

REFERENCES 189
MyCoach Interactive™ 193
Free Leadership Profile 194

CHAPTER 1

A Principal On Purpose: With a Purpose

Caught in a Campus Crossfire

I have been writing this book for more than ten years in my mind. When I decided to capture my thoughts on paper, it was hard to determine how and where to begin. After much anxiety, I thought about what my mother said when I did not know where to begin telling her a story. She would say, "Start at the beginning," and I would reply, "Okay, Mom, here goes."

MOTIVATING FACTOR

> *"Learn from yesterday, live for today, hope for tomorrow."*
> —Albert Einstein

My story is about my role as a principal and my journey to improve the schools that I had the privilege to lead. My story also includes my thoughts and research on systematic change, leadership coaching, effective leadership, staff development, adult learning theory, and an appeal to the leaders in America to *leave no principal behind*. I am passionate about the role principals play because they have the awesome responsibility for the success or the failure of our schools all over the nation. After twenty-plus years of actively serving as a principal, I am now retired, but I will always be a principal at heart.

There is something very special about principals. They tend to be born leaders who often take great risks. They care about the education of our youth and are attracted to the challenge of finding ways to make improvements in our schools. More often than not, the desire to make a difference is the motivating factor in the decision to become a principal. I know this was my motivation. I now know that desire alone is not enough–it has to be bolstered with something more.

I began my administrative career in 1970, as a Human Relations Specialist in the Oakland Unified School District in Oakland, California. My role required me to work with the principals of twenty-five schools, including one high school and its feeder junior high and elementary schools. Specifically, I was responsible for developing multi-ethnic classroom support materials and activities designed to create more harmonious relations between the many ethnic groups represented in that large urban school system. In addition, I was charged with creating an apparatus through which each school community could become more actively involved in the decision-making process at their school.

TURMOIL IN NATION

"Amidst the confusion of the times, the conflicts of conscience, and the turmoil of daily living, an abiding faith becomes an anchor to our lives."

—Thomas Monson

During that time, the city of Oakland and the surrounding cities in the San Francisco Bay Area were undergoing school integration; the Ku Klux Klan, the Hell's Angels, the Black Power movement, the Vietnam War, the hippies, the Black Panthers, and various liberation army movements were active, and there was overall unrest in the nation. I was attracted to the role of the principal because those very uncertain times in our history were challenging. I worked with principals day in and day out, and as a result, I gained an acute awareness of the enormity of the job. Subsequently, in 1973, I applied for a school principal position.

At that time, community involvement in the selection of school principals was the new strategy instituted by the new superintendent, Dr. Marcus Foster, and the Oakland Board of Education. Fifteen other candidates and I were interviewed by a thirty-member committee composed of school, district and community representatives. I was selected and began my career in school administration as the principal at Madison Junior High School, Oakland, California. I had the distinction of being the youngest principal selected in the history of the Oakland Unified School System and one of only a few females to head a secondary school in the system.

Very little real-life leadership support was given to me as I embarked upon my new role. It was equivalent to a non-swimmer being thrown into the middle of the ocean and told to swim to shore unassisted. I had to sink or swim.

FULLY CONFIDENT

"Who has confidence in himself will gain the confidence of others."
—Leib Lazarow

I entered school administration full of enthusiasm and ideas about how to improve the school. I felt confident that my years of teacher leadership, my master's degree in administration from the university, and the fact that I passed the state's competency test with a 95% average were all I needed to prepare me for this awesome and exciting career. I was ready to face the challenges, whatever they might be. I could never have been more wrong. Nothing had prepared me or readied me for what was to happen three months into my administration.

Nevertheless, I felt fully confident and sufficiently motivated to face the challenges, whatever they might be. After all, other colleagues were doing the job and were surviving, and so could I! Ninety days into my new job, I found myself in a life-threatening situation.

THE INCIDENT

"Success is not final, failure is not fatal: it is the courage to continue that counts."
—Winston Churchill

An inmate from a prison mental institution was released from incarceration. I was not informed by either the police department or by the district administration that he was to live in an apartment building just over the fence at the rear of my school campus. One day, he came onto the campus during the noon hour and, for reasons unknown, struck a teacher who was on yard duty. A number of students ran into my office to report that a strange man had hit one of the teachers. I shifted into safety mode. I immediately instituted a campus 'lock-down' and reported the alleged incident to the police department and to the office of Verdice Carter, the regional superintendent. I then proceeded with haste to the scene.

I summoned both vice principals and found that one was already on the scene, and I met him and the injured teacher walking into the building. The other vice principal was getting teachers and students into their classrooms for the 'lock-down.' We escorted the injured teacher into the counselor's office and called the school nurse to administer any needed medical attention. While she administered medical assistance, I took his preliminary statement. He told me that the man approached him and for no apparent reason made racial slurs to him, then struck him with a karate move and ran away. I told the one vice principal accompanying me to summon three of my most intimidating teachers— the head P.E. teacher, the shop teacher and the hall monitor— to join me in my office immediately after they escorted their students to the gymnasium.

When the three teachers arrived in my office, I instructed them to split up and cautiously sweep the campus, find the man and escort him to my office quickly and quietly. Meanwhile, the vice principals and I made sure all students and staff were safely behind locked doors. Shortly thereafter, the teachers found the assailant and brought him to my office. Not wanting to excite the man, I greeted him guardedly and asked him to sit down. He accepted my invitation by sitting in my chair at my desk. I was accompanied by the three teachers and both vice principals by this time. I proceeded to interview the assailant. As I questioned him, he began to use the papers on my desk to clean blood from one of his fingers. I tried to find out how he had injured himself, what his name was and where he lived, but could not get any intelligible answers. He ranted about how he had killed his dog and knocked out his apartment windows the night before. He also made several racial slurs. He continued ranting and talking about scenes from the movie *The Omen*, that recently aired on television. At this point, I realized this man was very dangerous.

POLICE ARRIVAL

"And thou wilt give thyself relief, if thou doest every act of thy life as if it were the last."

—Marcus Aurelius

To my relief, my secretary opened the door and escorted two police officers into my office. There were now eight people with the man in my office. It was getting crowded. Not wanting to overwhelm the man or get him more agitated, I released the three teachers and told them to return to the gymnasium and help the other teachers supervise the students there. I also told the vice principals to check the halls again to see that no students, teachers or parents were moving around the campus. We all felt reassured with the arrival of the police officers that everything was now under control.

SHOTS HEARD

"There are things that we don't want to happen but have to accept, things we don't want to know but have to learn, and people we can't live without but have to let go."

—Author Unknown

The officers began to interview the man in a very relaxed manner. He responded to them in the same manic mode that he reacted to my questions by giving a series of outlandish responses. After what I felt was a long while, I gave one of the officers a note that read, "Please remove this man. I have a school to run." The police officers then politely informed the man that they would have to leave so that the principal and the school could get back on schedule. The man abruptly stood up from my desk and walked to my conference room door. As they exited, one officer was in front of him and the other officer was behind him. I did not follow them because he was in police custody and I wanted to check on the staff and students. As the door closed behind them, I heard loud rumblings of conference room furniture being thrown around, some loud bumps against the wall, and a sound that went *Pow! Pow! Pow!* I exclaimed, "Oh my goodness! They had to kill the man!"

I dashed into the front office and told all office personnel to hide in the vice principals' offices and to lock the doors. I quickly ran across the hall to the cafeteria, where I used the phone to call the regional superintendent for the second time. This time I informed him that I heard shots, but I did not know the exact situation. I requested that he come to the school with additional support, but to use caution because I did not know what the situation in the conference room was at the time.

TURN OF EVENTS

"Courage is being afraid but going on anyhow."

—Dan Rather

After speaking with the regional superintendent, I went back through the cafeteria to see what was happening in my conference room. My intention was to get an update from the police officers regarding the shots we heard and to get the status of the assailant. I was stopped by one of the cafeteria workers. She was shaking and begging me not to go into the hall because she saw the man through a little window in the cafeteria door making karate moves near the front doors. It really did not register at the time that she said the man was in the hall and the police officers were not. To appease the cafeteria employee, whom I judged to be in a state of panic, I left through the rear door of the cafeteria and sprinted across campus to the gymnasium where a number of teachers and their students were in 'lock-down'.

HYSTERIA IN GYMNASIUM

"Fear cannot be banished, but it can be calmed without panic; it can be mitigated by reason and evaluation."

—Vannevar Bush

I entered the gymnasium and I saw everyone was in a panic. Both students and teachers were literally running from one end of the basketball court to the other, even my three most intimidating teachers. Someone shouted, "He's coming through this door!"

Everyone ran hysterically to the other end of the court. When they got to the other side, someone else shouted, "No! He's coming in through this door!" I was stunned that the teachers had not taken control of the situation and began to blow my whistle loudly and shouted to the teachers to lead the students into the bleachers, to get them seated and then I told everybody to calm down. I reminded them that they were behind locked doors and there was no reason to fear. I also told them that the vice principals had cleared the campus and everyone was safe.

After I restored order, I informed the staff and students that everyone was to remain behind locked doors until I gave the 'all clear' signal via the intercom. I left the gymnasium to return to my office. As I crossed the campus, I saw police officers chasing the assailant across the rear end of the campus, toward the apartment buildings with shotguns held high above their heads. When I saw the policemen chasing him, I thought that they were the same two officers who took the assailant from my office. I reasoned that they must have only injured him and he somehow got away from them and they were now chasing him.

THE GRAVITY OF THE MOMENT

> *"Life is not measured by the breaths you take,*
> *but by the moments that take your breath away."*
>
> —Author Unknown

I entered the back hall of the main building and proceeded to my conference room. I opened the door from the front hall and there, on the floor, were the two police officers —both had been shot in the head and were lying motionless on my conference room floor. The school nurse and the federal projects coordinator were kneeling at each officer, attempting to get a pulse. When they saw me, they told me that after they heard the shots, they ran to my office to find me, but found the police officers instead. It finally registered. The policemen lying on the floor were not the policemen who were chasing the man outside. In looking around the scene, I saw that the assailant disarmed one of the officers and shot them both in the head with a single gun. The other officer's gun was lying on the floor beside him. Suddenly I was overcome with the gravity of the moment–two police officers lay dead on my conference room floor; policemen chasing a deranged man outside my school; junior high school students and their teachers locked in the gymnasium and in the classrooms, and staff members who put themselves in harm's way to see that I was safe. It was a life-changing moment.

RUSH TO JUDGMENT

> *"Think like a man {woman} of action, and act*
> *like a man {woman} of thought."*
>
> —Henri Bergson

The regional office alerted the police department again after my second call to them and by now all the local television news stations were broadcasting about the shooting. Police cars, a SWAT team, district office personnel, hysterical parents, and community people stood behind police tape in front of the school. Helicopters swirled overhead. Two heavily armed police officers burst through the front doors and headed toward me as I stood in the conference room doorway speaking to my nurse and coordinator. One of the officers ran up to me, looked and saw the two downed officers and immediately took his weapon off safety. I heard the 'click, click' and looked around to find him lowering his aim toward my staff members still kneeling by the officers on the floor. Without thinking, I threw up my right arm, blocked his weapon and shouted, "No! These are my staff members! The man is running out that way!" These were staff members who had risked their lives for me. I was infuriated that the officer did not ask me about the situation and rushed to judgment by putting my staff in danger. I was annoyed that he did not assess the situation more carefully. Later, I learned that the police department used the incident at my school as a case study on how not to handle a similar situation.

STANDOFF AND CAPTURE

"None of us are responsible for all the things that happen to us, but we are responsible for the way we act when they do happen."

—Author Unknown

These two officers quickly left to join the others at the rear of the campus. Eventually, the assailant was captured in his apartment where he held a woman and her child captive in his bathroom. From the reports on the television news, he was wounded by a marksman after a long stand-off. Long after, I could still hear the awful sound of the rifle when the officer released the safety latch. I did not recall the feeling of fear or of panic. Everything seemed to happen in slow motion. It was as if I became a robot and moved through the entire incident automatically. Over and over again I recalled the details of the incident step by step. It was also then that I fully comprehended that the two fallen officers were deceased. These officers were our friends and were loved and respected by the school and the community. However, in my sadness, I felt relief that the students, the staff and I were safe.

THE ARMS OF MY SISTERS

"Is solace anywhere more comforting than in the arms of a sister?"

—Alice Walker

The district and regional superintendents were finally allowed to enter the building. I gave them my full report and informed them that the teacher who had been struck was okay. I recommended that someone take him to the clinic for a thorough check-up. I informed them that all students and staff were safe and still in 'lock-down'. The regional superintendent informed me that both of my sisters, Artis and Uline, also teachers in the system, were out front and wanted desperately to know that I was okay. I went to the front door and asked the officers to allow my sisters to come into the school. I let them know that I just needed to sit quietly with them and relax. I hugged both my sisters, we cried, and I felt a great sense of relief.

QUICK RECOVERY

"Have courage for the great sorrows of life and patience for the small ones; and when you have laboriously accomplished your daily task, go to sleep in peace. God is awake."

—Victor Hugo

The superintendents and I determined that we would release the staff and the students early that day. However, not wanting the events of that day to linger too long in our memories and disable us, I convinced the superintendents that we should continue school the next day. It was the right decision. We employed the use of several counselors and social workers to meet with students and staff. The students and the staff were supportive, and we returned to normal fairly quickly.

Surviving Neglect

PRE-SERVICE AND IN-SERVICE PREPARATION

"By failing to prepare you prepare to fail."

—Benjamin Franklin

The pre-service and in-service trainings that I received did not prepare me in any way for the events of that traumatic day. In urban and suburban schools all over the state, similar incidents were occurring, maybe not as tragic, but sufficiently serious enough. Many principals who find themselves in challenging situations are left behind to figure out how to respond to various situations unassisted and sometimes unprepared.

Leadership should be on purpose and with purpose; leadership should never be accidental. Leadership actions should be modeled on research-based best practices and not solely on intuition and survival instinct. While these characteristics are critical life skills, they should be coupled with the knowledge and skills required for the effective execution of the duties and responsibilities each job requires. For example, when a surgeon enters the operating room, she enters with many hours of ongoing surgical training. Her actions are on purpose, with purpose, to save lives. Principals deserve the same rigorous training when leading schools. Children's intellect and life success are at stake.

OUT OF NECESSITY

"Discontent is the first necessity of progress."
—Thomas A. Edison

To be clear, nobody forced me to choose school administration as either my profession or my vocation. The decision was mine. However, if I can get the attention of policymakers, staff developers and other principals by telling my story and sharing the lessons I have learned in my experience as a school principal, I will have fulfilled my mission.

I was sent into the inner city school's front line ill-prepared. I vowed that day that I would make every effort and seek every opportunity, on my own, to gain the knowledge, the skills and the competencies required of a school principal. I suppose the fear of the incident's repeating itself in one form or another was a great motivator for me to pay extra for my training, but I had no alternative at the time. The staff development offered by the district was not for my training and improvement; rather, it was for the dissemination of district policies, procedures and announcements. Sometimes we listened to different speakers and went on administrative retreats; however, the agenda remained virtually the same. Once in a great while I was allowed to attend a conference in another city, but the traditional staff development programs prevailed.

BECOMING MY OWN LEADERSHIP COACH

"If the wind will not serve, take the oars."
—Anonymous

Most of what I learned I disccovered for myself by reading books, reading research, listening to speakers, and attending conferences, however, it was not enough. If it had been, then I would not have felt the need for something more. Like early learning, we learn best by talking to others, watching others, asking questions, and exploring solutions. So I talked to leaders I respected and adapted many of the strategies that worked for them. I attended staff development trainings and extrapolated the content as it applied to leadership competencies. Most of the trainings were focused on effective classroom teaching strategies rather than on effective leadership, but I made them work for me. I researched leadership standards and competencies developed by different state departments of education, and compared my readiness to each of the major categories listed. I compiled a list of my strengths and weaknesses and asked myself what I must do to strengthen these skills. I researched leadership theories, styles and methods; talked to colleagues and supervisors; read numerous books by and about great leaders and what they did to become leaders of note. I literally became my own leadership coach without knowing that a leadership coaching discipline was emerging at that time.

In the early '70s, while on a fellowship assignment in Washington, D.C., I published an article titled "Women and Minorities in the Principalship: Career Opportunities and Problems." In the article, I call for more effective staff development for principals, especially for women and minorities. Recently, I've brought the need for targeted leadership training for principals to the attention of staff developers and district administrations. Some progress has been made since then, but not nearly enough.

DOCUMENTING THE COACHING PROCESS

"If you would understand anything, observe its beginnings and its development."

—Aristotle

Hence, in 1993, a full 20 years after I became a principal, I began to document the coaching process that I had been using, quite successfully, for my personal and professional growth, and incorporated it into the first version of my change model — the FLDS School Transformation Model™. I implemented the Model in a number of schools over the years. The process worked repeatedly as evidenced by increased test scores and improved school factors. On the basis of the success of my first model, I formed my first consulting firm and began using the Model to assist schools located in California, Kentucky, Chicago, Washington, D.C., and Texas. A number of the schools which implemented the Model with fidelity experienced growth and change.

THE BIRTH OF THE SCHOOL PRINCIPAL CHANGE MODEL™

"History does not repeat itself, but it rhymes."

—Mark Twain

In 1996, I revised the Model by updating the research on leadership coaching and school change, and it became the School Principal Change Model™. I implemented this new version for the first time while I worked on the Navajo Nation Reservation for the

Bureau of Indian Education. For four years, while I served as principal of Chinle Boarding School, Many Farms, Arizona, I implemented the Model as my vehicle for change. For three of the four years, the school improved in all major school factors as well as achieved adequate yearly progress (AYP) in the lower grades.

READING AS A SYSTEMS APPROACH

"Once you learn to read, you will be forever free."
—Frederick Douglass

In 2006, I became the principal of Shonto Preparatory School, Shonto, Arizona. During this time, the Bureau of Indian Education provided funds to schools for improving reading. I developed the job description, advertised for and hired two reading coaches to coach teachers in more effective teaching strategies. The reading coaches and I traveled to Harrisburg, Pennsylvania, to explore a program I had read about. There I found a process that would advance my goal of implementing reading as a systems approach to school improvement. After we returned from the conference, we developed a student-centered coaching process for Shonto Preparatory School.

For the ongoing professional development of my staff, I contracted with two consulting firms: One to provide staff development with ongoing training and coaching in reading literacy; the other to provide my staff with training in effective teaching strategies, as well as provide me and the reading coaches with an observation/feedback protocol.

In 2008, Shonto Preparatory School met the adequate yearly progress (AYP) benchmarks set by the State of Arizona in the areas of reading, mathematics and writing. The reading coaching strategies I chose improved my staff's teaching competencies, the same way that coaching had improved my leadership competencies over the years.

MY APPEAL TO OUR LEADERS IN EDUCATION

"An appeal to the reason of the people has never been known to fail in the long run."
—James Russell Lowell

My mission is to bring the coaching strategy for principal leadership into the full discourse on improving schools. My appeal to decision-makers at the highest levels is that no principal should be left behind for lack of a proven change process, such as the

School Principal Change Model™; and no principal should be left behind for the lack of a proven research-based staff development strategy, such as on-site leadership coaching. These two support systems will ensure that school principals develop effective leadership skills to meet the daily demands of our educational system. I believe we know how to improve schools. We need the collective will to do so.

My hope is that after reading this book, principals and staff developers will join me in the call for on-site, site-specific, and ongoing leadership coaching support as a permanent staff development strategy to assist principals in becoming more effective leaders.

CHAPTER 2

The 21ˢᵗ Century Challenge

"If your plan is for one year, plant rice; If your plan is for ten years, plant trees; If your plan is for a hundred years, educate children."
—Confucius

Removing Barriers

The challenge for the 21ˢᵗ Century is to make certain that every child gets the opportunity to attend a highly effective school. Highly effective schools do not just get that way. More often than not, they are led by highly effective principals.

The effectiveness of the principal, however, is often diminished as they are required to respond to a wide range of audiences and to an almost endless list of concerns such as:

- staff and student relations
- student discipline and staff violations

- social services and law enforcement issues
- health and safety needs of both staff and students
- reports and paperwork
- assessments and testing
- parents and community concerns
- policies, guidelines and requirements
- budgetary oversight
- facility responsibilities

One might argue that there are sufficient personnel to assist the principal; however, in the final analysis, the principal has ultimate responsibility for every decision made and every action taken on campus.

A NEW CALL FOR LEADERSHIP

> *"Change will not come if we wait for some other person or some other time. We are the ones we've been waiting for. We are the change that we seek."*
>
> —Barack Obama

Amidst the educational turmoil all across the nation, I am encouraged by what I see as a new call for leadership at all levels. President Obama's Blueprint for Reform in Education, the reauthorization of the Elementary and Secondary Education Act, and the Department of Education all assert that reforming our schools to deliver a world-class education is a shared responsibility – the task cannot be shouldered by our nation's teachers and principals alone. This affirms my belief that we must equip principals with the skills to develop school environments where teachers can impact student outcomes.

The President created the American Recovery and Reinvestment Act of 2009 (ARRA) as a fund opportunity to attend to significant needs in schools. This fund was designed to encourage and reward innovation and reforms that achieve significant improvements in student outcomes and substantial gains in student achievement in the areas of:

1. Improving teacher and principal effectiveness to ensure that every classroom has a great teacher and every school has a great leader

2. Providing information to families to help them evaluate and improve their children's schools, and to educators to help them improve their students' learning

3. Implementing college- and career-ready standards and developing improved assessments aligned with those standards

4. Improving student learning and achievement in America's lowest-performing schools by providing intensive support and effective interventions

It is important to note that the ARRA fund was not provided to all of the schools; it only granted funds for some of the schools. However, I am somewhat encouraged by that. While these were competitive funds and not all schools received them, I believe the goals set are applicable to all schools and should be adopted and incorporated.

The goals set in the ARRA Race to the Top initiative are steps in the right direction. The goals outlined in the framework are what I believe should be a national mandate to address the leadership needs of principals. Adopting these goals as a national mandate could ensure that each state would be held accountable for providing their schools, principals and teachers with the support they need to succeed, thus creating a shared burden where the accountability no longer falls solely at the doors of schools and school districts.

In reference to the first of the four ARRA goals above, the effort to ensure that every school has a great leader, will require the skills and talents of many because whether we have great teachers in every classroom and great principals in every school is leadership. In fact, research shows effective principals are the second determinant to positive impact on student achievement, and can improve the schools if they remain at the same school over a sustained period of time. Solving the education crisis requires focused attention on the professional development needs of the school principal.

BREAKING THE CYCLE

"Know Thyself."

—Socrates

For many school principals, admitting that we need help is often difficult. In general, leaders are reluctant to ask for help as they fear being perceived as weak or ill-equipped to lead effectively. I admit, from experience, that it was difficult for me to ask for help. However, I learned that such a simple and honest admission is a pre-requisite for change. It is the first step. Socrates is famous for arguing that one must Know Thyself to be wise, and that the unexamined life is not worth living. But how do we become wise? According to Confucius, "By three methods we may learn wisdom: first, by reflection, which is noblest; second, by imitation, which is easiest; and third, by experience, which is the bitterest."

The Lovelady School Leadership Coaching process attends to all three methods and enables principals to reveal their challenges and opportunities for development in conversations that are safe and in a supportive environment. Leadership coaching is about growth and change. It offers the opportunity for principals to modify behaviors that tend to interfere with the mission. Leadership coaching offers an environment for leaders to examine and change old patterns and habits that prevent us from reaching our full potential as leaders.

The homework assigned as part of the SPCM™ coaching process is designed to give principals an opportunity to implement the action plan, be self-reflective, practice new techniques determined in coaching sessions, implement strategies trained in the 5-phase SPCM™ change process and to build upon their own areas of expertise. The first step in this process is to admit to ourselves that we need to know and understand our strengths and weaknesses as leaders. We must make our leadership growth our goal. Tremendous benefits for both personal and professional growth are within our grasp. We need only to reach for them.

With the constant demands for accountability that steer the daily workload, it is difficult to find time to attend to our own leadership learning needs. But if we are going to break the cycle of neglect of leaders' professional development, then we must find the courage to say that we, as principals, just like our teachers and students, need support.

We are all familiar with the benefits of sports coaching. The coaches build teams, coach the athletes in skills improvement, build relationships, communicate effectively, instill discipline, and teach the team how to diagnose problems and find solutions. These are leadership skills that principals are also required to possess.

Sports coaches use playbooks and graphics to solidify team behavior. In football, for example, the players follow a systematic process and use strategies designed to score touchdowns. The entire team knows what to do when the quarterback calls for a certain play. The players are required to practice and memorize plays. They execute plays with precision until the whole team knows what to do, how to do it and when to do it. Sports philosophy and psychology have informed the executive coaching model, and research shows that coaching works in changing and improving behavior. Coaching makes winners. I argue that the coaching strategy works in leadership coaching for principals, too.

Schools also can benefit from the sports analogy by having a playbook. The School Principal Change Model™ is a playbook designed to create systematic and continuous improvement. It tells the school team what to do, how to do it and when to do it. Coaching and a systematic process can lead to success in schools, as in sports.

Most recent personnel selection practices require curriculum and instructional competencies for selecting school leaders. This addition has greatly improved the profession. However, what is missing is an accompanying work-related, ongoing professional development component to help principals attain and maintain these competencies. Staff development refers to the processes, programs and activities through which every organization develops, enhances and improves the skills, competences and overall performance of its employees and workers. The HR departments in most organizations, for example, are generally vested with the task and responsibilities of staff development. In school districts, however, this responsibility is often relegated to the Staff Development Departments or the Curriculum and Instruction Departments.

Ideally, the staff development plans chart out a staff development roadmap comprising training programs and initiatives to align with the organization's objectives and long-term organizational goals. I argue that the HR departments in our school districts should have total responsibility for training its workforce. Additionally, staff development should effect change in an individual's behaviors, values and beliefs. All too often, these elements are not immediately visible in many staff development designs, especially where principal trainings are concerned.

Few principals experience the benefits of leadership coaching because policies, practices and support are not uniformly adopted in school systems throughout the country. We must lead the call for this professional development opportunity. This is the opportunity for principals to explore what they already know, what they need to know and dialogue about, and how to translate this information into more effective leadership behaviors. This undertaking will change and improve leadership, teaching strategies, student engagement, and school outcomes. Everything we need is already available; we need only the will to act.

WHAT YOU NEED TO KNOW ABOUT CHANGE

"Action and reaction, ebb and flow, trial and error, change—this is the rhythm of living. Out of fear, clearer vision, and fresh hope. And out of hope, progress."

—Bruce Barton

We change only by changing. We cannot change schools until we change ourselves. Change is also a relational undertaking. We do this in schools by building strong collaborative teams. As we share strategies and ideas with each other, we gain from the collective wisdom of the group. We must bond, both in thought and behavior. Michael Fullan (2009) states, "Education is entirely about change – about drawing things out of people and creating the generations of the future. And effective change is inalienably about learning – figuring out the best way forward for the greatest good." It is my belief that change happens only through developing this kind of relationship with each other.

I made a conscious effort to recognize the needs of my staff by developing individual and collective relationships with them. When I entered a staff meeting, for example, I could feel the energy and know that the meeting was going to be easy or somewhat difficult. I was able to do this because I made the decision that none of the concerns were about me personally. My goal was to focus less on my needs and more on the needs of the team. Being a principal is a spiritual undertaking. Getting ready for it requires us to be unselfish. It requires us to work hard to make what we say match what we do. In other words, we become predictable. When our words match our actions, people begin to trust us. In the school setting, unless the teachers 'buy in' to our efforts to make change, nothing happens. I certainly found this to be true. It is therefore vital that we find ways in which we can become more trustworthy.

Principals can deepen their understanding about how to nurture and create a trustworthy environment by exploring their own motivations. Intrinsic motivation is deeply rooted in every individual and must be awakened through individual effort and desire. Leadership coaching is designed to help principals examine and clarify their values, beliefs, purpose, vision, and goals. In the coaching dialogue, the principals can pull from themselves a plan for their growth and change. Once the growth plan is determined, a coach can provide ongoing support during the implementation of this plan. This ensures that the principal has a greater chance for change and improvement. With the proliferation of demands on principals, setting and keeping these personal and professional priorities are ways I have found effective to change and break the crippling patterns that presently exist within the school bureaucracy.

Principals should understand that sometimes the fruits of their work may not be revealed until after they are gone. It is important, then, to leave the desire for change in the minds and hearts of the people. The goal of leadership is to induce others to embrace the mission with commitment and passion. After all is said and done, it is the people who will get the work done, anyway — not programs, not guidelines, not policies, and not mandates of any kind. It is in taking action that change takes place. If you can instill the desire to make things better long after you are gone, the process of change will continue in and by the people. If you are lucky, the organization itself will continue to change and grow in positive ways. If you are really lucky, the people will remember you and understand that your real motives were for the good of the organization. As it is often said, "If you give them a fish, they will eat for a day; but if you teach them to fish, they will eat for a lifetime."

PRINCIPAL WORK OVERLOAD

"Work is hard. Distractions are plentiful. And time is short."

—Adam Hochschild

We cannot successfully change schools without first addressing the tremendous workloads that principals carry. The duties of the principal have increased. Non-instructional activities fill the day and threaten to eliminate the opportunity to attend to instructional matters. With the many societal and political calls for more accountability, additional tasks have been added into the academic domain. As a result, the principals are required to respond to increased delegation from the national, state, district and agency-level policymakers. Everything is passed down.

The overwhelming workloads that principals carry in schools today prevent them from attending to the 'real' reasons for the school's very existence, which are curriculum and instruction. They make up the academic milieu for schools. Learning is about gaining knowledge. If principals never have an opportunity to organize the school in order to impart information, then students do not get to know or be able to do the things that will produce success for them in the future. That is why we are principals – to effectively teach students – not to be overburdened with busy work. Principals have to go through so many hoops to help students gain knowledge and information. Principals want to do better, but they need the time to do it.

For example, in my last principal role, from which I retired in 2011, I was required to supervise, observe and evaluate 76 personnel — a ratio of 76:1. The next highest manager-to-employee ratio in the school was in the Maintenance and Operations Department, at 36:1. There was even one department with a 1:1 ratio of manager to employee. This disproportionate ratio for me to observe, monitor and supervise my staff made it difficult to allocate time to my instructional duties.

In addition, I was required to perform all of the other duties and responsibilities listed in my job description approved by the Board of Education. I requested a workload analysis to address the work overload issue, but it never happened. Instead, I was ultimately assigned to manage the Exceptional Education Services Department — a new team of 12 — making my ratio 88:1. If anyone knows anything about special education services, there are an inordinate number of mandates, rules and regulations that require adherence.

Finding adequate time to allocate to instructional leadership duties was often my greatest challenge because every task required time for planning, organizing, implementing, monitoring and evaluating. My position description illustrates this challenge:

POSITION DESCRIPTION

TITLE:	K-8 Principal
EMPLOYMENT:	12 month, regular, full-time
SALARY:	Exempt Salary to be adjusted based upon the School Superintendent's recommendation
REPORTS TO:	Superintendent
SUPERVISES	All personnel in the K-8 School academic system (based upon the approved Table Organization)

QUALIFICATIONS

1. Candidates shall possess a Master's Degree or higher, with a major in educational administration or curriculum development.
2. Candidates shall possess a valid Arizona School Principal Certificate; or eligibility for same.
3. Candidates who have advanced technology skills shall be given preference.
4. Candidates must have a thorough understanding of the teaching/ learning process.
5. Candidates should have at least two years' experience in school administration and supervision.

6. Candidates should have at least two years' successful experience as a classroom teacher.
7. Candidates having experience with or support of standards-driven curriculum are preferred.
8. The district supports the Navajo Preference in Employment Act, but will consider candidates who are not Navajo.
9. While an applicant may appear to possess the necessary minimal qualifications, it will be the candidate's performance at an interview, as determined by the Superintendent, which will determine whether or not a candidate is qualified for the position.
10. Successful completion of all interviews, background checks, and fingerprint clearance requirements, and submission of all employment-related documents and forms.
11. Such alternatives to the above qualifications as the Board may find appropriate and acceptable.

PERFORMANCE RESPONSIBILITIES

1. Establishes and maintains an effective learning climate in the school.
2. Programs classes within established guidelines to meet pupil needs.
3. Supervises the academic guidance program to enhance individual student education and development.
4. Establishes guidelines for proper student conduct and maintaining student discipline.
5. Supervises the school's teaching/learning process.
6. Plans, organizes, and directs implementation of all school activities.
7. Initiates, designs, and implements programs to meet specific needs of the school.
8. Establishes and maintains favorable relationships with local community groups and individuals to foster understanding and solicit support for overall school objectives and programs; interprets Board Policies and administrative directives; discusses and resolves individual student problems.
9. Orients newly assigned staff members and assists in their development as appropriate.
10. Coordinates and supervises support services such as building-related maintenance, security, food services, recreational programs, financial and accounting functions, library activities, etc.
11. Works actively with the Teacher-In-Charge of Exceptional Education Services to provide a comprehensive program for gifted and special education students.

12. Coordinates and supervises the school's athletic and extracurricular programs, where applicable.
13. Evaluates and counsels staff members regarding their individual and group performance.
14. Prepares or supervises the preparation of reports, records, lists, and all other paper work required or appropriate to the school's administration.
15. Participates in the O.B.N. meetings, personnel meetings and such other meetings as are required or appropriate.
16. Prepares and submits the school's budgetary requests and monitors expenditures of funds.
17. Attends special events held to recognize student achievement and attends school-sponsored activities, functions, and athletic events.
18. Maintains and controls the various local funds generated by student activities.
19. Cooperates with the Curriculum and Professional Development Office regarding teacher training and preparation.
20. Works with various members of the central administrative staff on school support problems, such as transportation, residential dorms, special services, and the like.
21. Conducts staff meetings to keep members informed of policy changes, new programs and the like.
22. Keeps the Superintendent informed of the school's activities and problems.
23. Keeps abreast of changes and developments in the profession by attending professional meetings, reading professional journals and other publications, and discussing problems of mutual interest with others in the field.

As the position description demonstrates, the duties are overwhelming, even for an effective principal. There just is not enough time in a day or even a school year to complete all of the duties assigned. I am highly organized and had processes and procedures for everything we did. I had a cooperative staff that did things systematically. I created internal support systems and hired outside consultants. Still, I could not execute all duties to meet my standards of excellence. After an examination of several school principal position descriptions from other school districts, I found many similarities to the job description assigned to me. The number of duties and responsibilities were virtually the same, confirming the pervasiveness of the problem.

Not only is the principal's workload increasing in the United States, it is rising in other countries as well. Some of the most frequently cited challenges facing school leadership in Ireland relate to work overload. In a 2005 Survey of Secondary School Principals conducted by Joint Managerial Body, more than 90% of principals stated that dealing with legislation significantly affected their work.

According to Grady, et al. (1994), data gathered on Australian school principals and their professional and personal backgrounds showed that the major reasons most principals intended to retire five years early related to pressure of the job (41%), schools being asked to do too much (30%), additional work responsibilities and/or employee termination (23%).

Vandenberghe, et al. (2003) reports on the dissatisfaction, severe workloads, and the overburden of Flemish elementary school principals. The report indicates that an important number of principals believe they lack the competencies to live up to the performance standards that have been set; that too many different tasks prevent them from completing their jobs; and that the environment in which the school and its principal must function offers little support. As the three research studies above show, the workload issue for principals spans several countries. Even so, little has been done to change it.

Further complicating principals' efforts to deliver top-quality instruction are national education policies that tend to change when a new administration takes office. The national education reforms drive new policies, programs, grants, projects, funding, and new requirements for each state, district and local school site. With all of these changes come additional legal responsibilities and requirements. Principals have to lead the school from the previous educational guidelines and requirements while they try to understand the new standards and ensure adherence. Principals have to ensure effective implementation down to the classroom level and, at the same time, balance the daily demands from the students, teachers, community, parents, school boards and district administrations. From my experience, it is no easy task to transition from one change to another without help and support.

Is it any wonder, given the issues that I have discussed, that the American education system is in crisis? Schools are failing. Our children deserve better. I have dedicated my entire professional career to education and I refuse to accept this condition. The question then is: What do we do?

Policymakers at all levels who are genuinely interested in making a significant impact on student achievement can do the following:

1. Implement an organizational workload analysis to ascertain whether there are a disproportionate number of duties assigned to principals. The workload analysis will also be used to discover whether some of the non-instructional duties can be assigned to other departments within the organization.

2. Conduct an examination of the professional development content and delivery system to uncover whether or not principals are receiving ongoing real-time coaching support for their leadership skills and competencies.

3. Conduct an examination of the budget to establish whether funds are adequately allocated to provide ongoing fiscal support to professional development leadership coaching for principals.

Based on the research findings cited, although not conclusive, principals suffer from work overload, lack of competencies that could be mitigated with leadership coaching support, and complicated legislation. I wonder if anyone who is not a principal understands the magnitude of the job duties assigned to the school principal. Principals desire to meet the demands that the system requires, but cannot meet them all with the same degree of success without support.

CHAPTER 3

What Leaves Principals Behind?

"Education is at the turning point."
—Howard Gardner

Changing Tradition–A New Paradigm

One motivation for my writing this book is to initiate a discussion about how I think principals are left behind in the search to improve schools. I do not claim to be an empirical researcher; however, what I do claim to know are the negative consequences the following factors had on my ability to lead schools more effectively. Throughout this book, I discuss reasons principals are left behind, and I offer a solution that worked for me. In this chapter, I discuss four structural reasons: 1) organizational culture and tradition; 2) budget priorities and allocation; 3) leadership impact on student learning, and 4) staff development program design.

ORGANIZATIONAL CULTURE AND TRADITION

"The definition of insanity is doing the same thing over and over again and expecting different results."

—Albert Einstein

School culture is a set of norms that make up the persona of each school, and each school is different. If the school culture is misunderstood, then determining what needs to be changed is problematic.

Hargreaves and Fullan (1994) assert that there are four distinct cultures in educational institutions: isolationist, balkanized, contrived collegial, and collegial. They suggest that educational institutions have a long tradition of isolationism, with the entire educational system operating within its own small environment. If we isolate ourselves, we become trapped within our own limited beliefs, preventing other influences from enabling us to have greater insights to transform. Hargreaves and Fullan further suggest that this isolation accounts for many of the failures we see in schools. Only when we reach out and interact with other entities do we grow and understand the larger educational picture.

Principals operate in what Douglas Reeves (*Change Wars*, 2009) calls a culture of "command and control." Reeves describes this culture of "command and control" as a 19th-century business management strategy that has failed. Distinguished more by popularity than by effectiveness, this leadership practice was standardized by leaders in early American automobile manufacturing companies. Despite ineffective results, these practices are well maintained in the business environment as well as in today's educational leadership practices.

Traditionally principals were, in large part, hired because of their autocratic leadership style. These principals were guaranteed tenure as long as they could keep their staff and students under control. For many years, I worked as a principal in this environment and I have seen how this style of leading has become integrated within educational institutions. It is very much a part of the school organizational culture today. While there is much research in literature that states that the autocratic leadership style produces diminishing returns, the practice prevails.

Peterson (2002) suggests that school culture is responsible for the way members of the school [school district] regard themselves, relate to each other, and view the institution goals (Diaz-Maggioli, 2004). The members within the education culture are so isolated that they often do not consider more innovative ways of training and maintaining its workforce, and as such, contribute to their own failure. Even though research informs us that collaboration and interaction, or what some refer to as professional learning communities, produce change and transformation within schools, the traditional autocratic leadership style and isolated culture thrives. As a result, the ongoing professional development needs of the principal go unnoticed.

Educational leaders and policymakers at the top management levels practice and perpetuate the "command and control" tradition. They do this by dictating change at the top and by expecting said change to trickle down for principals to implement in schools. Since the success or failure of any initiative lives or dies at the principal's desk, a routine exclusion of the principal from reform initiatives by top-level decision-makers means that little or no implementation will take place. Yet the practice of excluding the principal from the decision-making process continues and results in a pervasive resistance to change at the school level. Until policymakers and upper management abandon the "command and control" philosophy and include principals in the conversations about how best to change and improve schools, the principals will be left behind and schools will continue on a path to failure.

BUDGET PRIORITIES AND ALLOCATIONS

"The development of a tree depends on where it is planted."

—Edward Joyner, Yale University

This quote expresses my philosophy about budgeting. It means that support for instruction should be 'planted in the budget'. For example, in developing my budgets for each school year, I always involved my staff in a budget needs assessment process. I asked that my teachers request items in such major areas as equipment, books, materials, technology, furniture, and trainings for the upcoming school year. I based my priorities on the analysis of the needs assessment. The first round of requests was dedicated to individual teacher needs, as some teachers requested items unique to their teaching styles. The second round of requests was dedicated to items that all teachers would use to uniformly deliver instruction across the curriculum. I prioritized the needs based on the goals and objectives set in our school improvement plan. The result of this process ensured that at the beginning of each school year the teachers had everything they needed to support the teaching and learning process.

Budgets should always be about priorities. In building my school-level budget, I first sought input from my teachers. Second, I prioritized the needs and made sure that they correlated with our school goals and objectives. Third, I allocated sufficient funds. I considered it my responsibility to find out what teachers needed; I 'planted' those needs in the budget, and then saw that everything was ordered, delivered and disseminated for their instructional use.

I believe that school budgets should be built from the classroom level up. Similarly, I believe that districts should build their budgets from the school level up. For example, in preparing the budgets for leadership staff development, if districts would simply make it a practice to ask the principals what they need, many principals would agree, that in doing so, principals would be more inclined to support reform initiatives proposed and they would have the appropriate funding needed for their ongoing leadership professional development.

According to the National Center for Education Statistics, the current expenditures for approximately 98,000 public elementary and secondary schools is about $540 billion for the 2010-2011 school year, and projected to be about $566 billion for the 2011-2012 school year. Principals lead the institutions that train our future generations, and in today's environment of dwindling school resources and budget cuts, improving the leadership capability of the principals carries increased significance as it is vital to the survival of our nation. It is crucial that policymakers recognize the value and return on investment gained from allocating the appropriate dollars to what research has proven to have a direct impact on student achievement.

LEADERSHIP IMPACT ON STUDENT LEARNING

"Do first things first, and second things not at all."

—Peter Drucker

This quote holds great meaning for me. Mr. Drucker reminds me, as I struggle to place the professional development needs of principals at the top of the national agenda, how easy it is to continue to do what is familiar and comfortable, and how difficult it is to tackle the highest priority.

Numerous research studies have demonstrated the positive correlation between a school's leadership and the academic achievement of its students. One such analysis of 69 studies illustrated below – involving 2,802 schools, 14,000 teachers, and 1.4 million students – showed that improving an average principal's leadership by 34% usually results in a 10% increase in student academic achievement in that principal's school. Similarly, a 49% increase in leadership ability predicted a 22% academic achievement increase over time.

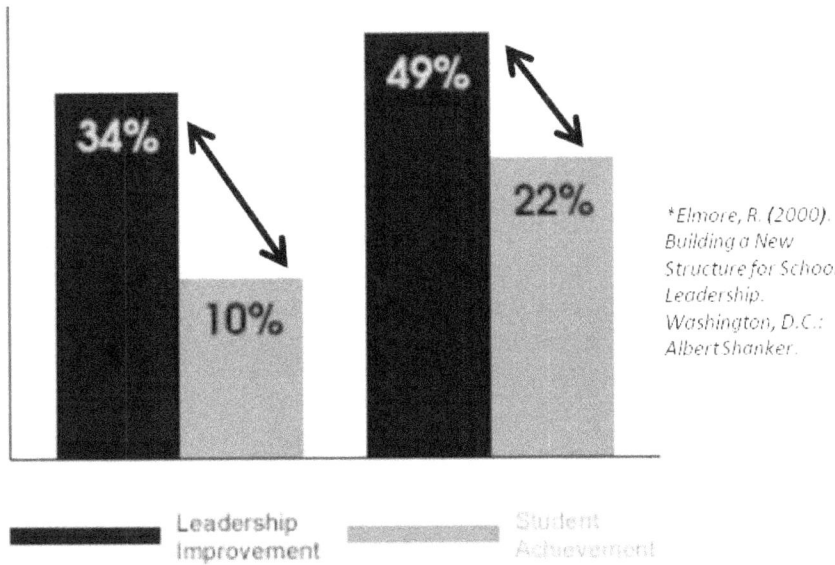

The potential to increase academic achievement through developing principal leadership skills is significant. This study provides the evidence that leadership has a direct impact on student achievement. Additional research shows that school leadership has a substantial effect on student learning. Salazar (2008) states that nearly 25% of the in-school factors affecting student achievement can be attributed directly to the quality and effectiveness of the principal. The fact that principals interview, select, manage, support, develop, and evaluate teachers means that the quality of teacher instruction is significantly dependent on the effectiveness of the principals. Yet, we continue to deprive principals professional development support.

STAFF DEVELOPMENT PROGRAM DESIGN

"If you do what you've always done, you get what you've always gotten."

—Tony Robbins

The majority of trainings are focused on two components: the presentation of theory, and the inclusion of some demonstrations. Research shows that coaching is the best method for learning a new skill, and it shows that it is the best method for transferring skills into the workplace. Most of us would agree that the goals of staff development are to change individuals' knowledge, understanding, behaviors and skills; however, the two components currently used for leadership development practices are conventional and insufficient to meet those goals.

According to Joyce and Showers (2002), five components are necessary for training to be effective for skill acquisition and use. They include theory, demonstration, practice, feedback, and follow-up or coaching. These components are defined as follows:

- **Theory**. Presentation of the theory or rationale that defines the value, importance, and use of the skill. Often, this is what looks and sounds like a lecture or the equivalent of direct instruction for students. It is the telling or describing portion of training.

- **Demonstration** or modeling of the skill, typically by the trainer.

- **Practice**. Opportunities for learners to practice the skill, both while under the direction of experts, and over time in more natural settings.

- **Feedback**. Timely and constructive feedback on learners' practice, so they can understand what they are doing well and what needs further refinement.

- **Follow-up or coaching**. Long-term guidance and assistance so that what was practiced in training sessions or other simulations is transferred to the actual work setting.

In a staff development training no one component of the Joyce and Showers model causes transfer into classroom [workplace] use. Only with the gradual addition of all training elements, and in particular, coaching, will transfer into classroom use [workplace use] occur.

While this study was conducted on teachers, the implications for leadership professional development are strong. The Joyce and Showers research was about teacher behavior change. There is no reason to believe then that coaching at the leadership level will have any less impact on leadership behavior. It should have the same level of impact on behavior in the workplace as it does in the classroom. Joyce and Showers (1995) state, "this gradual addition of training elements does not appear to impact transfer noticeably…However, a large and dramatic increase in transfer of training occurs when in-class coaching is added to an initial training experience comprised of theory, explanation, demonstrations, and practice with feedback." Without follow-up or coaching support over time, the transfer of skills into a routine in the classroom or workplace is reduced or does not happen at all. Note the effects of transfer of training when coaching is added:

	Training Outcomes		
Training Components and Combinations	Knowledge	Skill	Transfer of Training
Theory	.15	.50	.00
Theory, Demonstration	.66	.86	.00
Theory, Demonstration, Practice	1.15	.72	.00
Theory, Demonstration, Practice, Feedback	1.31	1.18	.39
Theory, Demonstration, Practice, Feedback, Coaching	2.71	1.25	1.68

Tallerico, M (2005)

Bush (*Effective Staff Development*, 1984) conducted a study to test the efficacy of the five components included in this Joyce and Showers model. His study confirmed that coaching is the critical factor in effecting a change in the skills of a large number of people. Bush examined how the components contributed toward skill transfer or the development of new behaviors into classroom practices. He corroborated the gradual addition of the five components by testing the number of people who transferred knowledge and skills, showing that no one component is enough. Bush's research of Joyce and Showers' theory showed that the first 4 components resulted in 16-19 out of 100 people able to perform the new skill in the classroom. However, when the coaching component was added, up to 95 people transferred the skill into practice.

Significant research, like the studies above, have accumulated over a number of years.

Showers, et al. (*A Synthesis of Research on Staff Development*, 1987) organized the literature and provided highlights of the existing body of research on staff development in a meta-analysis of nearly 200 studies outlining:

- What the teacher thinks about teaching determines what the teacher does when teaching. In training teachers, therefore, we must provide more than "going through the motions" of teaching.

- Almost all teachers can take useful information back to their classrooms when training includes four parts: (1) presentation of theory, (2) demonstration of the new strategy, (3) initial practice in the workshop, and (4) prompt feedback about their efforts.

- Teachers are likely to keep and use new strategies and concepts if they receive coaching (either expert or peer) while they are trying the new ideas in their classrooms.

- Competent teachers with high self-esteem usually benefit more from training than their less competent, less confident colleagues.

- Flexibility in thinking helps teachers learn new skills and incorporate them into their repertoires of tried-and-true methods.

- Individual teaching styles and value orientations do not often affect teachers' abilities to learn from staff development.

- A basic level of knowledge or skill in a new approach is necessary before teachers can "buy in" to it.

- Initial enthusiasm for training is reassuring to the organizers but has relatively little influence upon learning.

- It doesn't seem to matter where or when training is held, and it doesn't really matter what the role of the trainer is (administrator, teacher, or professor). What does matter is the training design.

- Similarly, the effects of training do not depend on whether teachers organize and direct the program, although social cohesion and shared understandings do facilitate teachers' willingness to try out new ideas.

The research confirms that whether relatively simple teaching skills or complex curricular or instructional models or leadership training are the object of the training, the first four components appear to increase knowledge, skills and the probability of transfer to the classroom or the workplace for a short period of time, but only when coaching was added as a component did the teachers keep and use the new skill. These findings have significant implications for coaching as a strategy to increase leadership competencies.

Despite the well recorded and reported research about effective staff development, the majority of staff development programs for principals do not include coaching support. This inadequacy in leadership training leaves principals behind.

In this chapter I talked about what I believe leaves principals behind:

1) the organizational culture and tradition of "command and control"

2) the lack of evidence of leadership training as a budget priority

3) the disregard for the findings that leadership correlates with student achievement, and

4) the lack of leadership coaching as part of staff development and program designs

When combined, it is overwhelmingly evident that eliminating only one factor will not solve the problem. We must address all of the mitigating factors in order for the leadership needs of principals to become a top priority.

Three major themes emerge from the foregoing discussion:

1) Coaching is the only staff development component that changes behavior
2) The repositioning of staff development, especially for principals, is needed and should be reflected as a priority in budgets
3) The design of leadership staff development should be tailor – made to fit the real-life work of the principal

I am calling for staff developers and decision-makers at the highest levels to remedy these deficiencies.

CHAPTER 4

The School Principal Change Model™

How It Works

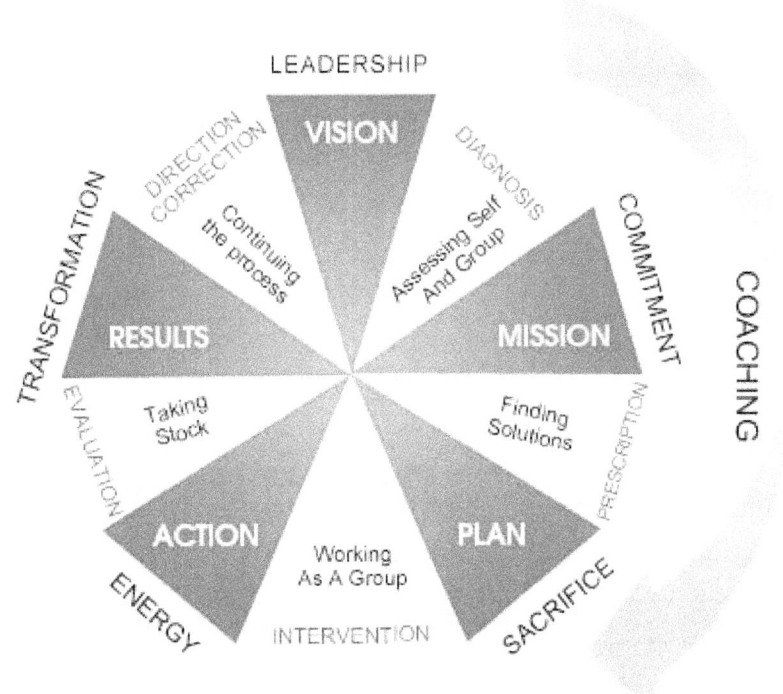

The School Principal Change Model™ (SPCM™) was organized with the assumption that change is incremental and does not take place at once. Change seldom happens all at once. The

Model represents a series of intentional actions that, when implemented with fidelity, will increase a school's chances for permanent change and transformation.

The concept of the SPCM™ is based on the work of Dr. W. Edwards Deming, who is considered by many to be the father of modern quality control. It also borrows from ideas rooted in the Scientific Method. The SPCM™ is a systematic and interactive change process that provides leadership coaching for principals. I developed and tested this model while working as a principal. I used it repeatedly as a remedy for the everyday challenges I encountered in my efforts to impact teaching and learning. I offer it as a remedy for other principals to use to systematically address change in their schools.

To establish the model, I implemented the following steps: 1) selected the change process and leadership coaching as areas of focus; 2) collected data on each approach; 3) organized the data by counting the instances of successful outcomes; 4) analyzed, interpreted, and adjusted the Model as the data dictated, and 5) determined the most appropriate actions and made them permanent phases with related steps within the process. Each phase was systematically implemented, observed, documented and replicated in different school settings over a ten-year period.

The SPCM™ contains five phases. Within each phase are required actions, activities and behavior characteristics. The five Phases address the major stages in the School Principal Change Model™ process. The five Characteristics address the personal qualities that a school principal must possess as an effective leader of change. The five components address the major modules that must be implemented, and the five Group Activities address the major tasks that the principal, staff and parents must implement to activate the change process.

The following table displays the contents contained in the 5 Phases of the SPCM™.

Phase	Characteristic	Components	Group Activity
Vision	Leadership	Diagnosis	Assess Self and Group
Mission	Commitment	Prescription	Find Solutions
Plan	Sacrifice	Intervention	Work as a Group
Action	Energy	Evaluation	Taking Stock
Results	Transformation	Direction Correction	Continue the Process

Leadership, Vision, Assessing Self and Group, and Diagnosis constitute **Phase 1**. I have combined leadership and vision here because visionary leaders activate the staff's imagination to what the future could be. The Assessing Self and Group, and Diagnosis components combine to provide the baseline data from the principal leadership assessment and the school stakeholder assessments. The data from these assessments form the database from which all future decisions will be made.

Commitment, Mission, Finding Solutions, and Prescription constitute **Phase 2**. Commitment is the mindset needed to successfully accomplish the mission. In this Phase, the school leadership team and the principal explore and determine the school's purpose. The Finding Solutions group activity produces many ideas that can be captured in the Mission Statement. Once the exploration for solutions is accomplished, the principal and the school leadership team will organize the solutions into prescriptions designed to remedy the mitigating factors that impede progress within the school.

Sacrifice, Plan, Working as a Group, and Intervention constitute **Phase 3**. This phase is labor-intensive because a large amount of school time and staff voluntary time is required to explore and determine which prescriptions will be recommended at the conclusion of the work in this Phase. The written plan becomes the official written document known as the comprehensive school plan. This plan includes the goals, objectives, responsibilities, timelines, and evaluation methods that will be used to determine success. The second document produced in this Phase is the Strategic Action Plan. The Strategic Action Plan includes all of the action tasks that will be required to implement the written plan. These two plans are sometimes combined into one document. I find that it is more efficient to have one plan that tells what work has to be done, and another to tell how the work will be done. One or both of these documents are sometimes required submittals to the district and other agencies.

Energy, Action, Taking Stock, and Evaluation constitute **Phase 4**. It is within this phase that dormant forces within the organization tend to surface. They surface whenever there is movement that will change the status quo. These forces resist change. If they are not identified and eliminated, they hold the potential to derail the school team from successfully completing the mission. Fortitude and resilience are attributes required in this phase because the resisting forces are, more often than not, institutionalized within the organization itself. The principal and the school leadership team must exert equal or greater energy than the resisting forces if change is to occur. Ongoing and careful monitoring is essential to ensure that the actions stay on course to produce the intended outcomes reflected in the mission statement. Taking Stock is a monitoring strategy, and Evaluation is a program assessment strategy. Both are used to give the school improvement team valuable information about how well they are doing and whether or not they need to refine or eliminate certain strategies that are not working. Sometimes this requires the elimination of entire programs.

Transformation, Results, Direction Correction, and Continuing the Process constitute ***Phase 5***. This is the final phase designed to provide evidence that change has or has not occurred. Since we know that change is a constant, the change that the principal and the school leadership team are looking for is whether the predicted outcomes were accomplished. Transformation and results reflect the changed behaviors within the organization. The principal and the school leadership team use the information gathered from the evaluation to correct and change the direction in which the entire school team is going. If the findings show that little or no progress has been made on certain goals and objectives, new objectives and tasks are planned and the process continues in a cyclical fashion.

If, on the other hand, the team finds that many of the milestones were accomplished and student benchmarks showed improvement, then the process continues and momentum is maintained. If, for any reason, the school district determines that an entirely new reform direction is required, and it is one that carries the schools in a totally new direction, the initial momentum, gained by systematic implementation, will be interrupted and chances are high that the school will revert to its original state and growth will be interrupted.

It is therefore important that the district administration determine what the schools are doing that works and include those successful programs and strategies as part of the new direction.

Phase 1: Vision

CHARACTERISTIC: LEADERSHIP

"Great leadership requires great vision."

—F. Lovelady-Spain

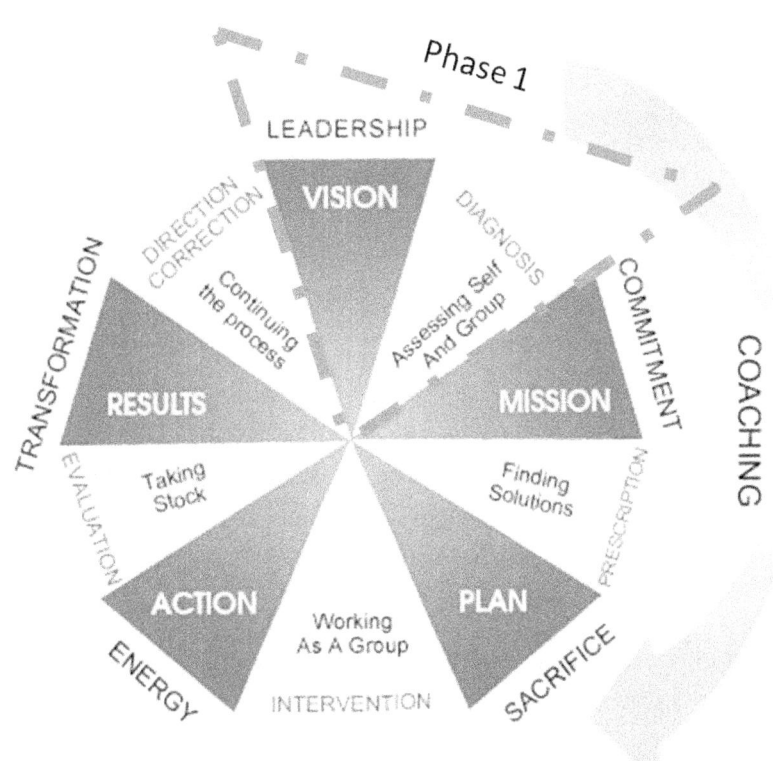

Phase 1, *Vision*, begins with the Leadership characteristic. At the core of leadership is vision. It is important that the leader possesses the ability to convey a clear picture of their vision so that it takes root in the minds of others. Taking proven actions and strategies will transform schools. Effective leaders communicate a vision and induce others into action.

I first learned about vision from my mother. I frequently think of her describing her vision to me about what she wanted for her children. I remember her telling me that when she was 13 years old, she worked in the cotton fields. She labored long and hard in the hot Texas fields for a pittance. Oftentimes, to help the family make ends meet, she had to work instead of going to school. One day, she said, her future became crystal clear to her. She told me that she leaned on her chopping hoe and promised herself, "When I have children, I will do whatever it takes to send every one of them to college to get an education so they will never have do this kind of back-breaking work." Of her seven children, all went to college. While in college, all of my four brothers were drafted and served honorably in the military. They all returned safely and four of us received doctorates. My mother's vision for me and her other children was realized. I have never really worked in the cotton fields as a permanent means to make a living.

I recognize that my mother's vision has been manifesting in me throughout my life experiences. Groomed for leadership from an early age, I believe I was destined to be a school leader. Throughout my school years, I was appointed and elected to leadership positions, and I was often recognized for outstanding achievement. The student body, for example, elected me into numerous leadership roles throughout my high school years, and one of those positions was President of the National Homemakers of America Club. This was a statewide club organized to provide leadership training to young girls. I was later elected to President at the local, district and state levels. At that time, I played basketball and was in the marching band. I was one of the star girls' basketball players and received the all-'round medal upon graduation from high school. In addition, the band director selected me as assistant band director because I could read music and had learned to play a "mean" trombone. Even today, after 50 years, I am still recognized for leadership roles I held in high school. In 2010, I was inducted into the Sports Hall of Fame by the city of Rockdale, Texas, my hometown.

In college, I took a significant leadership role in the civil rights "sit-in movement" sweeping college and university campuses around the nation. My sorority sisters of Delta Sigma Theta recognized my willingness to fight for change and selected me to run for president of the student body of Texas Southern University in Houston. I did not win, but the experience sharpened my leadership skills and helped shape my leadership philosophy.

I have learned leadership skills from research and practice, mistakes and successes, and from observing effective leaders. Every leadership lesson I have learned up to this point is contained in the School Principal Change Model™. It is a character-building and competency-building experience that begins with establishing a clear vision.

You might ask, "What is vision? How can you tell a visionary leader when you see one?" One way to understand vision is to define it. Vision expresses the method an organization or a school uses to gaze into the future. Vision is a long-term outlook describing how the school would like to be. Vision requires discernment and perception.

I have come to learn that visionary leaders activate the imagination to what the future could be. A visionary leader is one who is committed to a core set of values, and these values are embedded in a sense of personal integrity.

Mahatma Gandhi, Martin Luther King, and Nelson Mandela, each visionaries in their times, promoted non-violence and envisioned a future where skin color would not be a barrier. Gandhi envisioned the day that his people would be freed from colonial rule; Martin Luther King envisioned the dream that one day his children would be judged by the content of their character and not the color of their skin. His children saw this vision realized on November 20, 2008, when Barack Obama became the first African-American president of the United States of America. Nelson Mandela, who endured 27 years of imprisonment and non-violent protest, envisioned a nation that could exist without apartheid. Upon his release from prison, Mandela became the president and leader of that same South African nation that incarcerated him as a political prisoner.

Several key research studies discuss leadership characteristics and skills needed for the 21st century and beyond. Effective leadership is two-dimensional, affective and cognitive – both domains are important in a professional development program. The following researchers discuss the characteristics, skills and importance of effective leadership.

Warren Bennis (2003), in his book *On Becoming a Leader*, forecasts the behaviors necessary for leadership in the 21st century. He maintains that modern leaders must not rely only on their personal skills or charisma to produce change. He identifies four critical characteristics of effective leadership. First, leaders must be able to engage others through the creation of a shared vision. Second, leaders must have a clear voice that is distinctive to constituents, and this voice should be characterized by a sense of purpose, a sense of self and self-confidence. Third, leaders must operate from a strong moral code and a belief in a higher good that fuels their efforts. Finally, leaders must have the ability to adapt to relentless pressure to change.

Peter Block (2003), in his book *The Answer to How Is Yes: Acting on What Matters*, describes leadership as the act of effective questioning. Block suggests that the leadership skills of convening critical discussions, naming the question, and focusing the discussion on learning rather than premature closure on solutions are necessary in solving organizational problems.

Jim Collins (2001), author of *Good to Great*, a work that has influenced both business and education, suggests that the difference between "good" companies and "great" companies is the presence of what he refers to as Level 5 leaders. Collins elucidates that Level 5 leaders are concerned about building a great company and not in personal glorification. They combine personal humility with intense personal will. When things go wrong, they tend to look inward for the reasons rather than attribute the blame to external factors.

Stephen Covey (1989), in his signature work, *The 7 Habits of Highly Effective People*, hypothesizes seven behaviors that lead to positive results in a range of situations. He outlines these habits as instructions: Be proactive; Begin with the end in mind; Put first things first; Think win-win; Seek first to understand and then to be understood; Synergize; and Sharpen the saw. His second work, *Principle-Centered Leadership*, builds on his seven habits as the basic operating principles of effective leadership.

There is something transcendent about vision and visionary leadership. The best way I can explain having vision is to compare it to having faith. Faith is commonly described as "the essence of things hoped for and the evidence of things not seen." This means that what you can imagine now and act upon with diligence is what will manifest in the future.

The visionary school leader establishes a mechanism to accomplish the future, reflected in the school's vision statement. They are clear about the particular steps necessary to get there. They have a clear sense of the direction in which they want the school and education to go. Visionaries are people who are able to inspire.

The ability to increase one's visionary leadership is a learned skill. It can be accomplished by learning to balance the mental, emotional, physical, and spiritual dimensions. The School Principal Change Model™ combines with leadership coaching to facilitate the principal's opportunity to increase visualization abilities. With growth and change in the dimensions listed above, the principal becomes empowered to expand his or her insight. Visionary leadership, in the context of this book, is one that is focused on effective instructional leadership that promotes more effective delivery of instruction in the classroom.

This leadership propels others into attitudes and actions that manifest in the spirit exhibited by the students and the staff, as well as in the culture and the climate of the school, by communicating a sense of pride and of community. The behavior codes, the communication patterns, and the values that the school cherishes are easy to see and quantify. What the school organization values and believes is conveyed through what is said and done consistently within the school.

When I went to Shonto Preparatory School, I gave my staff the following components that characterized my vision for the school:

- Shonto Preparatory School is a school where teachers are constantly engaged in staff development trainings that renew and provide research-based instructional strategies
- Data is used to inform leadership and teaching decisions
- Coaching is used as a strategy to reinforce, guide, support, and provide observations, feedback, and reflection to teachers
- Collaboration is the preferred means of communication
- Sharing of best practices, both horizontally and vertically, across grade levels is standard practice
- Standards-based curriculum is mapped, unwrapped, paced, monitored and evaluated
- Research-based student engagement strategies are used for instruction and interventions
- Leadership is shared by staff, students and parents
- Fidelity to the programs and program designs is school-wide

I envisioned a school where the staff, the students and the parents understood what we were doing, why we were doing it, how we were doing it and how well we were doing it. To accomplish the components of my vision, I implemented the School Principal Change Model™ and incorporated the S.A.I.L.S. process as a way to focus on Curriculum, Instruction and Assessment. S.A.I.L.S represents the following major goals:

- Standards
- Assessment
- Instruction and Interventions
- Leadership
- School-wide Commitment

In 2006, and every year thereafter for five years, I displayed the S.A.I.L.S. process on the front hall bulletin board for all to see. As we began our School Principal Change Model™ continuous improvement process, the S.A.I.L.S. acronym was symbolized by small boats floating across a vast ocean. As our achievement scores increased year after year, the small boats became ships, then tankers, then huge battle vessels. In this way, I was able to keep the vision alive and the focus on instruction. The bulletin board motivated staff and students, and communicated our goals to our parents and all who entered our building. In fact, one of the members of the National Commission on Accreditation (NCA) who was assigned to evaluate our school commented that it was easy to tell what our goals were from looking at the bulletin board. Eventually, students, staff and parents were able to tell others about our program and how well we were doing by observing the size of the ships.

Like Mahatma Gandhi, Martin Luther King and Nelson Mandela, I, too, had a dream. My vision was of what I wanted my school to look like and what I wanted it to become. I organized my action plan to accomplish that dream. My staff and I were faithful to it. We took consistent actions, we accomplished our intended results, and were rewarded for our hard work. My K-8 school received superior ratings in virtually all of the NCA accreditation standards.

Advancing through Phase 1, the diagnostic process provides the foundation for Phase 2 – Mission. The diagnostic information is the evidence that the principal, the school improvement team, and the parents will use to create the mission statement in Phase 2 of the School Principal Change Model™.

The *diagnosis* component is implemented after the vision statement has been finalized.

It includes an assessment of the personal leadership skills of the principal and is designed to create several leadership profiles used in one-to-one coaching of the principal. It also includes the assessment of the entire school organization as a group. In the diagnostic process, both formative and summative assessments are used to collect information. The evidence found in the diagnostic process can also be used to correlate with the state standards, which identify what students need to know and be able to do.

Just as doctors diagnose for information that tells them about their patient's condition, schools also diagnose for information that tells them about the leadership, teaching and students' academic needs. The diagnosis will reveal what the strengths and weaknesses are in the organization. This is the beginning of the change process. It enables the staff and parents to establish the baseline data from which the mission statement, the written plan, and actions plans are developed.

Phase 2: Mission

CHARACTERISTIC: COMMITMENT

"A great mission requires great commitment."

—F. Lovelady-Spain

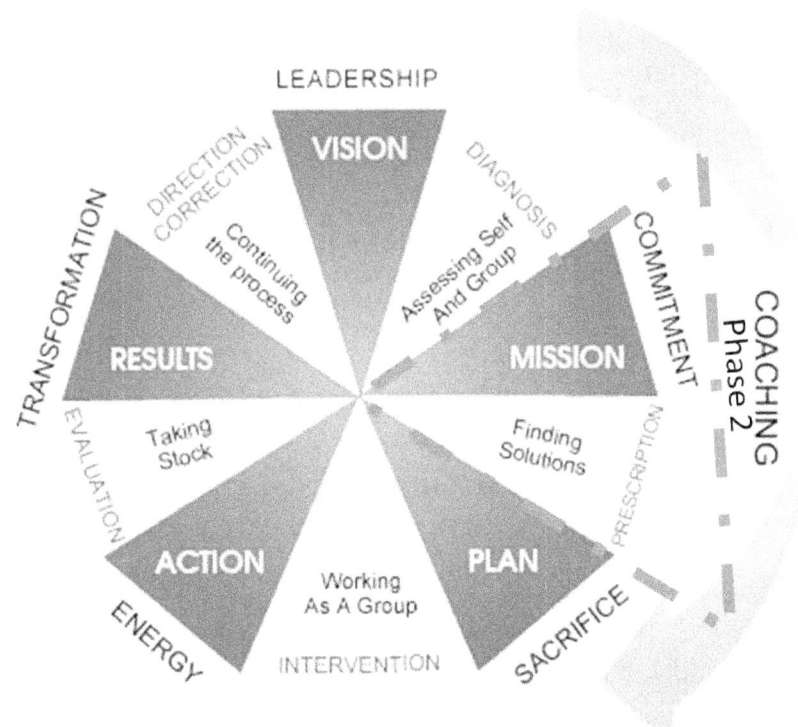

Once all of the assessments from Phase 1 are selected, scheduled, disseminated, completed, collected, analyzed and translated, the school leadership team can begin Phase 2 – *Mission*. This phase includes developing the mission statement, building commitment, writing the prescription, and finding solutions.

The principal begins this phase by leading the school through a mission statement development process. The mission statement is a brief description of a school's purpose. A sample mission development process is provided in Chapter 8: Tools, Techniques and Other Resources. The mission statement explains why the school exists and what it does to achieve its vision. The mission statement provides details of what will be done. It answers the question, "What do we do?" For example, your mission statement may read, "The school will provide standards-based curriculum." It articulates the purpose to the stakeholders.

It is important to note that two major activities and their implementation are integral parts of mission statement development: *Prescription,* and *Finding Solutions.* The leadership coach can provide significant support to the principal in this area of the process.

The principal should present two guiding questions to the leadership team. The answer to "Where do we want to be?" begins the prescription development. The answers to "How do we get there?" initiate the finding-solutions stage of the Model. To expand on the answers, it is important for the principal to lead the team through a series of exercises to:

- Help them think of all the possible things that can be done to move closer to achieving the goal
- Break down any large steps into smaller components so the team sees that the objectives are achievable

As part of the exercise, the principal asks the team, "What are the biggest obstacles?" and "What could go wrong?" and leads them through a brainstorming exercise to explore how they might eliminate the obstacles identified. Sub-committees are formed right away to begin eliminating as many of the obstacles as possible. Left unattended, these obstacles can derail the work of the school's mission.

Once the mission statement has been developed and the obstacles have been eliminated, the team identifies the major goals and objectives. The goals and objectives need to be clear, challenging, and stimulating enough to motivate the staff to stretch, but not be so challenging that they will cause stress.

Once the goals and objectives have been established, the school leadership team is ready to set timelines and responsibilities. This step helps establish the length of time to spend accomplishing certain objectives, and who is delegated to perform the tasks. Beginning with objectives that can be started immediately, the school team lists the benefits the school organization will gain by achieving the goal(s). There is little point in having a plan that starts in three months' time; loss of momentum is the risk.

For many years, as principal, I used the School Principal Change Model™ as a continuous improvement framework in which I coached my staff through every phase of the model. Documented evidence showed that each school, though different and in different parts of the country, improved. The improvements were school-wide and in all areas of the curricula.

An effective leader commits to the possibilities of change even though there may not be any clear indication of its happening. The leader must build a framework in which commitment can grow. Commit comes from the Latin word meaning "to bind together." One might ask, "How can one build commitment?" From my experience, I have learned that building commitment happens when you focus on the needs of others before your own.

For example, my first principal assignment was to an urban junior high school in Oakland, California. The school was located in a middle-income African-American neighborhood. Most of the parents worked and had high expectations and hopes for their children's education. The student population was 99% African-American. The ethnic make-up of the staff, however, mirrored the district's ethnic make-up at the time, which was about 1/3 African-American, 1/3 Caucasian, and 1/3 Hispanic/Asian/Pacific Islanders. The neighborhood had a reputation for drug trafficking and use. In fact, it was later revealed in an HBO television special that one of the most notorious drug dealers in America, at that time, resided in a nearby community. Student disciplinary incidents were high and, on occasion, gang members would enroll in the school and cause chaos both in and out of the classrooms. My students had to walk past a liquor store every day to get to school. The staff was talented yet apathetic, and did not believe much change could happen. I was told that the former principal's car had been jacked and the wheel severed, causing the car to fall to the ground when he got in it to drive home.

Amidst all these factors, my first challenge was to build a team that would commit to a set of goals that would improve both student and school outcomes. My second challenge was to earn their trust. I had to prove to them that I would follow through with some of their identified needs and wants.

Anticipating that my staff's first priority was to improve the academic performance of the students, I scheduled a staff meeting in which I presented the academic achievement data covering a three-year period. My colorful and detailed chart reflected the achievement trends in reading, math and science. It was easy to see that the trend lines basically remained the same, reflecting little or no growth across the board. Looking at my chart, my first question to my staff was, "What do you think the first priority should be at our school?" Instead of offering solutions to the low achievement, my staff wanted to know what I was going to do about the boys wearing hats in the building. They also wanted to know what I was going to do about the awful appearance of the faculty dining room. Both issues were supported rather energetically by most of the faculty.

I must admit that my head started to spin, my mouth felt like it dropped to the floor, and I had a flash-back to a television series called *Diff'rent Strokes*, in which one of the characters would say, "What you talking 'bout, Willis?" when he was confused. All of these things happened in my head, of course, and thankfully I did not verbalize my surprise nor did my body language betray me. I ceremoniously placed the chart with the very low test scores to the side and immediately began to problem-solve the two issues raised by the staff.

We formed two committees, one for the hat issue and one for the faculty dining room issue. For both issues, we set meeting dates, held several meetings, brainstormed possible solutions, presented the recommendations during the next staff meeting, and obtained consensus from the entire staff. We set a short timeline of two weeks for the hat issue, and one month for the faculty dining room issue. Essentially the hat policy was determined as follows:

- Those teachers who did not want the students to wear hats in their classes received my support and the support of the administrative staff. We held a meeting with each affected class and made sure that the students honored the wishes of the teachers during the appropriately assigned class periods. The two vice principals and I assigned ourselves to cover all class periods.

- Those teachers who did not mind hats were an easy fix. It turned out that in private conversations with most of them that they cared more what was in the heads of their students than what was on the heads of their students. That was refreshing to hear.

In addressing the faculty dining room issue, to my great pleasure it turned out to be a school-wide project. The ultra-talented art teacher volunteered to be the chairperson.

First, he obtained a color swatch booklet and arranged for the staff to check off their color choices. Second, he recruited the metal teacher, whose students created a hanging lamp and flower hangers as a class project; the woodworking teacher, whose students painted the walls and door frames; and the home economics teacher, whose students chose a corresponding color for the curtains, sewed them and mounted them at all the windows. It took the committee about a month to complete the project. Finally, he planned a celebration and sent out engraved invitations that his art students created. We were set for the 'Grand Opening' of the newly renovated teachers' dining room.

The cafeteria department prepared a fine breakfast, staff members dressed especially nice for our early morning shindig, our home economics students served us, the superintendent and his deputy were our guests, and we all enjoyed our really Red dining room with rose window curtains, table cloths, hanging lamps and plants. The woodworking teacher carved a sign for the door that read 'Club Madison.' I thanked him and told him I would hang it in my office to remind me of my first year as principal. I did not tell him that I did not want the parents to get the wrong idea about what our focus really was. The red dining room was beautiful but sufficiently surprising enough to our parents.

I immediately scheduled a special staff meeting and once again held up the test scores and asked the question, "Now, what do you think our first priority ought to be at our school?" My entire staff in unison said, "To raise our test scores!" I responded, "Then, let's just do it!" I gained their trust and from that day forward, my staff and I were committed to a common vision and a common mission for our school. Eventually, the State of California recognized us as a model school. This is just one story about building commitment. I am sure there are many additional stories that can be shared.

The mission statement has to be alive in each person in the organization. It needs to be embraced one by one until all stakeholders are deeply rooted in it and it becomes their passion. It is a personal commitment based on deep regard for children, their future and the betterment of the American school system. The mission statement needs to be embedded in the very fiber of our being and become the reason for waking up in the morning. It is the motivator for working hard all day.

It is necessary to make a distinction between a vision statement and a mission statement. The vision focuses more on what is going to happen in the future. The mission statement focuses on what needs to be done now. Both statements are important because they allow everyone in the organization to know where the school is going and what the school must do now to get there. It takes commitment to stay focused on both the vision and the mission.

Effective leadership requires that we make a professional obligation to see that the responsibility for schooling is sustained by the whole team. It requires a specialized set of relational skills. These skills are used to ensure that others in the school organization are motivated and able to work together to carry out the school's vision. The leader keeps her or his eye on the vision of the organization and makes sure that everyone within the organization does what needs to be done to attain that vision. In this respect, the leader is not so much the driver of change within the school, but the catalyst for change.

At the completion of Phase 2 – Mission, a celebration is planned to acknowledge the commitment shown by the entire school team. The reward can be in the form of an ice cream social or anything that is fun and expresses appreciation for the long and dedicated hours they spent. The work accomplished here will form the basis for Phase 3 – Plan.

Phase 3: Plan

CHARACTERISTIC: SACRIFICE

"Great plans require great sacrifices."
—F. Lovelady-Spain

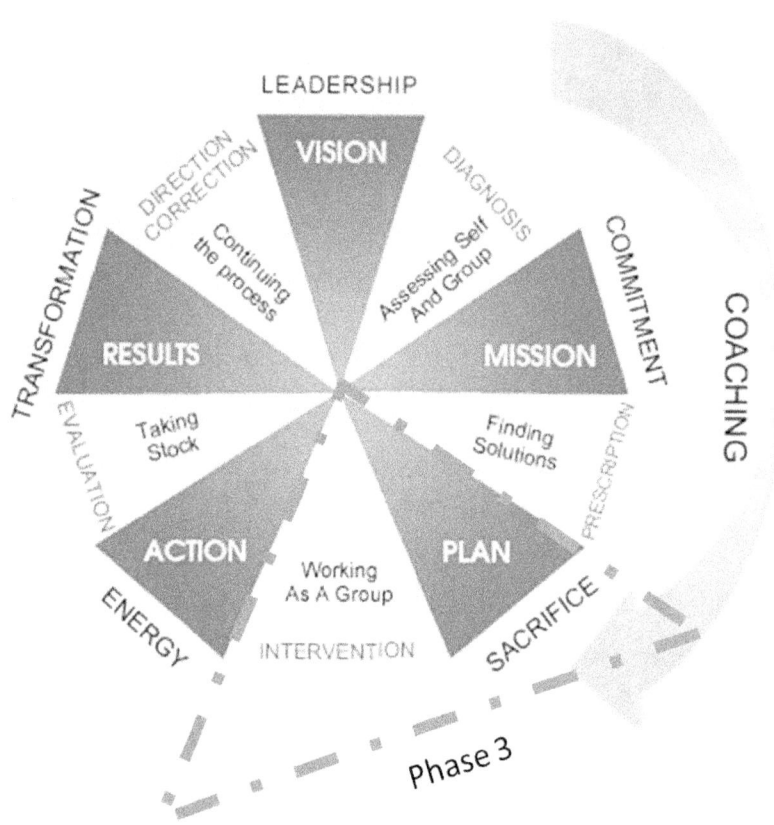

Phase 3 is *Plan* development. The Plan is the written documentation of the prescription or remedy determined by the work of the school improvement team in Phase 2. The Plan requires adequate time to do research, to collaborate, and to reach consensus on chosen strategies that will be organized into the comprehensive school plan document. The plan requires the school team to organize the objectives and the tasks in logical and chronological order. It requires that the principal and the school leadership team set weekly, bi-weekly or monthly goals. It spells out the required research necessary to successfully accomplish each task. All of the actions in the plan require timelines stipulating when the tasks will begin and when they will end.

Numerous committees and sub-committees will *work together as groups* to organize their work. These committees and sub-committees establish their own protocols for the work completion. The protocols may stipulate such things as ground rules for members, how the meetings will be facilitated, how decisions will be documented, the length of time allocated for the meetings, when meetings will occur, how often meetings will be held, where meeting will be held, and deadlines for completing certain milestones. The planning process takes time and requires sufficient energy for thoughtful completion. I recommend that each committee build into their routine certain physical exercises designed to energize their members. Having healthy snacks such as fruits, nuts, raw veggies and juices are also advisable. Different members can volunteer to bring the snacks from week to week.

In planning, two important steps will be accomplished. One is the strategic planning and the other is project planning.

First, strategic planning is a process by which an organization completes and documents, in written form, a comprehensive plan for moving the school's goals toward the long-range vision. The strategic plan identifies long-range school goals as well as high-priority projects to pursue over the next 2-5 years. Strategic planning takes into consideration all identified school needs. It requires four steps:

1. Selecting and analyzing data on the performance of children from different demographics within the school
2. Making reasonable assumptions about the future
3. Translating those assumptions into goals and objectives
4. Implementation

There are several advantages to strategic planning. It engages the entire community in preparing for change, it captures the goals of the school community in an orderly and efficient manner, it encourages the school community to share in the achievement of the goals, and it promotes the efficient use of the school and community organizational resources.

Second, project-planning addresses how specific needs and goals identified in strategic planning will be accomplished. For example, in curriculum development, the project planning may result in the identification of all the necessary tasks required to implement a comprehensive curriculum development process. The project plan culminates in the preparation of the main objectives in each part of the school for the implementation of the comprehensive curriculum development process. The project planning process addresses the specific needs and goals for which budget will be allocated. It is necessary then in project planning that the overall strategic plan is consulted and reviewed carefully and often.

At this stage in the change process, leadership coaching of the principal can be of tremendous benefit. The discussions thus far have been in the realm of ideas. Now the principal and the school leadership team are required to take action. The principal will begin to face resistance from the organization, and the coach can help the principal manage the change process. The coach will keep in mind that the following factors may be present in efforts to move the principal forward:

- *Self-concept* and *self-esteem* are reflections of past experiences and may affect the principal's willingness and ability to cope with change
- *Stress and anxiety* levels may be heightened when the principal feels threatened in any way
- *Past experiences*, values, beliefs impact on how we receive new information, and coaches must value these experiences, but if they are keeping the principal from moving forward, the coach needs to identify and discuss the limitations of the principal's current knowledge and skills.

When a school plans, they must dare to dream by starting with a statement of the perfect school. Alternatively, if the focus were more specific, then making a statement of the optimal condition for the school would be appropriate. For example, a school may envision a community where all the children graduate from high school; there are no dropouts; a large percentage of graduates go on to some form of higher education; funding is sufficient to provide assistance to these students so that they can attend the school of their choice, and so on. Planning takes great sacrifice on the part of the entire school community because time is required to sufficiently complete the steps of the School Principal Change Model™. To culminate the work of the committees and sub-committees, each committee will submit a list of interventions that will be implemented in Phase 4, which involves taking action.

Phase 4: Action

CHARACTERISTIC: ENERGY

"Great actions require great energy."
—F. Lovelady-Spain

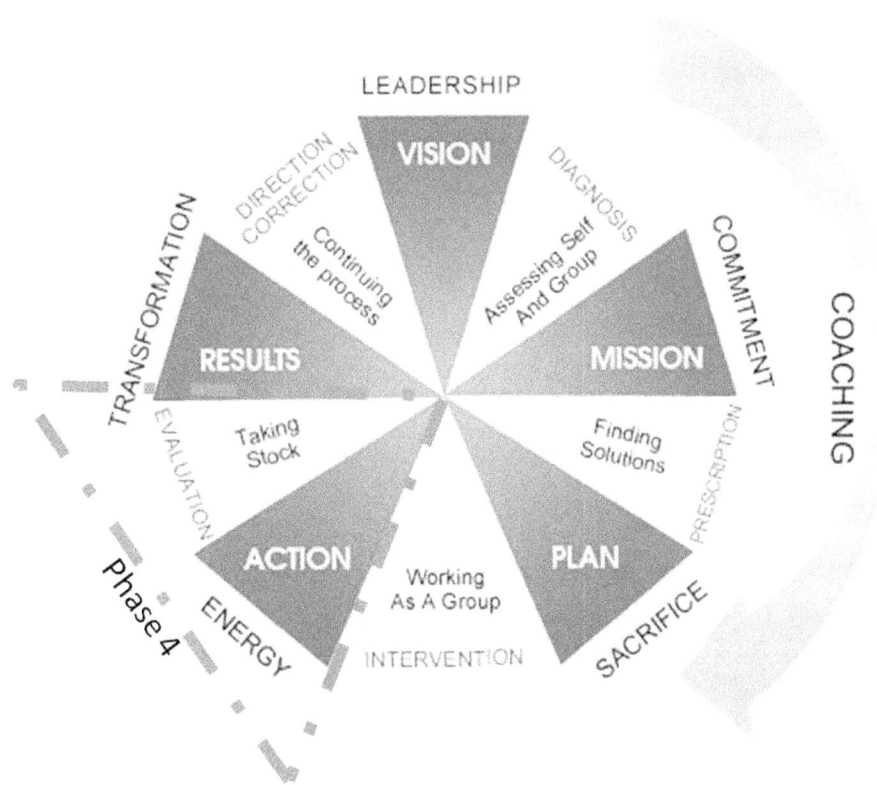

Phase 4 is about taking *Action*. Taking action is considered the most important step in the School Principal Change Model™. The actions taken by the principal, the staff and the parents are critical to the success of the mission. In the action phase, many forces are at work, forces that have the potential to derail the effectiveness of the entire school organization.

The seeds of destruction of any good idea currently exist within the school itself. These seeds are referred to as resisting forces. They tend to lie dormant until actions are taken to change things. They immediately spring into action all by themselves. Each organizational structure has a level of resistance, and the school organization, as far as I have experienced and observed, has the greatest level of resistance to change.

The following explanation for this phenomenon is brilliantly demonstrated by Joe Petterle (1993), in his book *Schools Flunk…Kids Don't*. Dr. Petterle suggests that those who seek change follow a basic pattern of:

MISSION ➡ PLAN ➡ ACTION = RESULTS

"The mission or desired outcomes drive the plan which, in turn, drives the action or changed behavior," says Petterle. "When all goes well, this changed behavior brings about new or changed results. These results are tangible indicators, the assessment, that the mission is being accomplished. Unless the projected results are clearly spelled out and correspond directly to the mission, change will not occur. It is the projected results that motivate changes in behavior – "Assessment drives change."

Dr. Petterle further asserts that most plans fail. He states that most plans fail because they neglect one key piece of the puzzle, the existing environment. The tables below represents his idea:

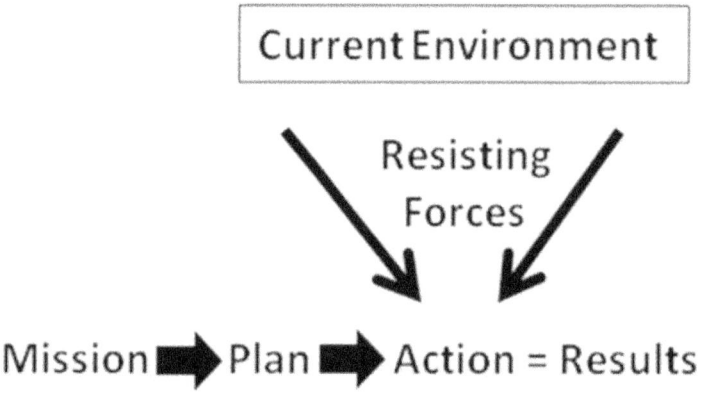

The resisting forces exist within the current environment. They lie dormant until the point of action. Next, I show how the forces take certain forms when they learn that change is taking place:

The School Principal Change Model™: How It Works 75

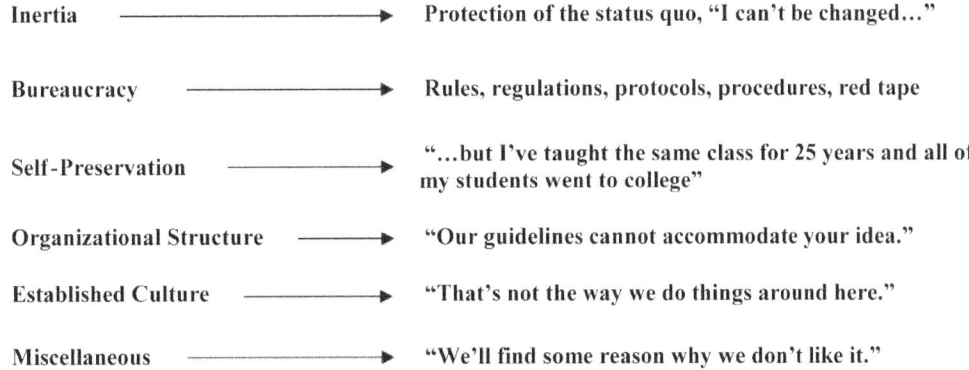

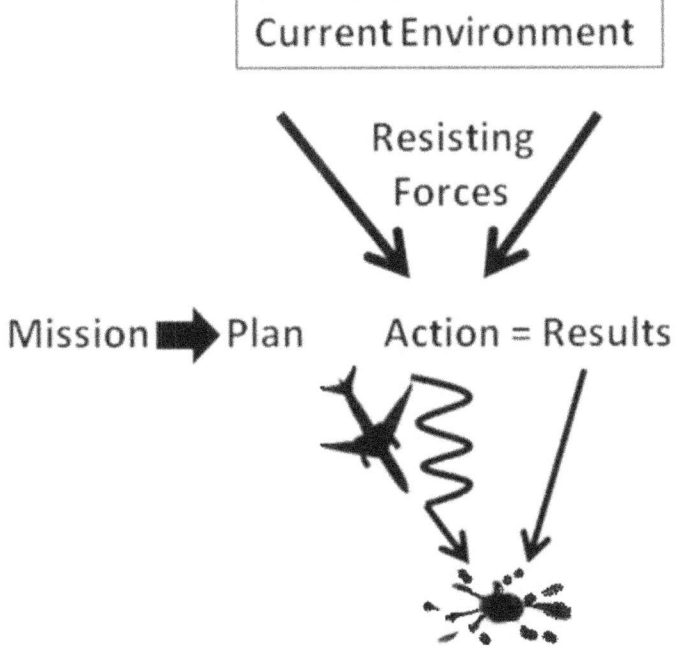

It is important at this point to state that the resisting forces are not premeditated and are not some scheme dreamed up by members of your combined staff. The resisting forces make up the complex interactions of well-intentioned professionals doing what they think is best for the school and the children. You might ask then, "What is a leader to do, if there are no bad guys that can be identified?" Don't give up just yet; there is a way to push ahead.

I have found that too few leaders spend adequate time identifying the obstacles that can cause plans to fail. In the foregoing discussions in the Mission phase and in the Plan phase of the School Principal Change Model™, I urged you to brainstorm as many obstacles as could be identified. These obstacles represent the resisting forces. By simply asking "How can this obstacle cause our plan to fail?", you implement the process referred to as 'failing your plan'. In other words, the identity of these obstacles reveals to you who and what the resisting forces are. Now all that is required is to determine how to eliminate them. For those institutionalized resisters, such as the bureaucracy, set it aside until a strategy can be developed to prevent it from causing your plan to fail. Continue with the instructional change process.

If the school or school system wants to do a more comprehensive Total Quality assessment, I found the work of Dr. Kent Stephens to be transformational. Dr. Stephens (1970) conducted research on Failure Avoidance Technology. His research resulted in the development of the Sage Analysis, which predicts and graphically depicts where and how a plan or new idea will fail. There will be instances when your staff may want to know why you are spending so much time talking about negative things and talking about failure. To address these concerns, Dr. Stephens offers, "What is more positive than avoiding failure, and how can you avoid it if you don't understand it? How can you understand if you don't analyze for it?"

Dr. Petterle explains the Sage Analysis as a graphic depiction and prediction of where and how a plan or an idea will fail. He goes on to say that in a school, this means that as you set in motion a plan to bring about substantive change, you also predict where the plan will meet resistance and what will cause it to fail to live up to its expectations. He further states that you must identify the resistance and trace it through the cause-effect logic to its source, and then you can develop counteractive strategies and integrate them into your strategic plan. He concludes his explanation by stating that you must not only create a strategic plan, you must also "failsafe" its implementation. For example, the Sage Analysis graphic representation of cause-effect logic for low attendance will be represented in a chart similar to the one below:

                       Because of…

                   Because of …

Low Attendance in our school is Because of…

                    Because of…

                        Because of…

The principal and the leadership team can greatly facilitate the Action phase by taking the steps to avoid failure.

Taking action is orchestrated by the school principal. The principal, using the strategic plan developed by the entire staff, will provide both the written and verbal instructions on how to carry out particular change initiatives. The strategic plan will contain the goals, the objectives, the persons responsible for implementation, how the plan will be implemented, whether or not the goal was implemented successfully, and to what degree. The principal is responsible for clarifying and orchestrating the basic implementation instructions of the strategic plan, keeping in mind that there will be other areas within the school that will be a part of the whole instructional focus.

When I became principal of Shonto Preparatory School in 2006, I found that there was no systematic alignment of the reading program or of the strategies used to teach reading across the grade levels. This missing component contributed to the school-wide failure in reading. During the month of July, I analyzed three years' worth of the AIMS reading test scores. I was particularly interested in the reading scores because research has found – and I concur – that reading is the foundation to success in education and in life. Thus, the leadership focus for the first year of my administration became reading.

I organized my findings into a presentation and introduced it to the superintendent, the administration and the Shonto Board of Education during the Summer Board Retreat. I titled the presentation "Reading As a Systems Approach to Student Achievement and School Improvement." I set forth the rationale, the research, and plan to improve student and school outcomes.

When the staff returned for the start of the new school year, I showed this same presentation to them. Hence, I made it clear to the staff that one of my goals was to improve student achievement in the reading content areas by strengthening the teaching of reading and the strategies we chose to do so. A presentation can be found in Chapter 8: Tools, Techniques, and Other Resources and can be downloaded from MyCoach Interactive™ at www.LoveladySchoolLeadership.com for you to use with your team.

Next, I developed a comprehensive 'Principal's Action Plan' designed to guide my leadership actions in the implementation of the reading goal. The table below shows the beginning steps I took to implement the reading curriculum project. These steps are partial and not intended to be exhaustive. I include them only to provide an example of the detailed thinking and steps required to orchestrate a goal:

PRINCIPAL'S ACTION PLAN

Goal: To implement research-based reading programs at all grade levels

Task What is the objective?	Talent Who is responsible?	Timeline When will it begin?
Contact the Director of Curriculum and Instruction and request that we obtain several research-based reading programs from various vendors for examination by staff.	Principal Director of Curriculum	August 15, 2006
Determine the location and set-up space for the reading programs display, keeping in mind that the display will remain for an extended period of time.	Principal Dean of Students	August 22, 2006
Develop a schedule with beginning, ending and selection dates	Principal Master Scheduler	August 29, 2006
Develop the evaluation criteria to be used during the review of each reading program.	Principal Reading Coaches Curriculum and Instruction Director	August 30, 2006
Schedule a staff meeting to discuss and disseminate schedule and evaluation criteria.	Principal	September 3, 2006
Tally the results, discuss the merits of each program and select the reading programs for the K-5 lower grade levels and the 6-8 upper grade levels	Principal Entire Staff	September 15, 2006

To conclude the discussion on Phase 4 - Action, remember that the main aspect in preparing an action plan is to have clear objectives. Ask the question "Where do I want to be?" To be motivating, the goal needs to be challenging enough to stimulate the entire staff into enthusiastic action. It should ask the teachers to stretch their skills bank and challenge themselves to take learning and teaching to new heights.

It is important to look at the steps and determine whether they are logical and in chronological order. I used the "Triple T" model (Task, Talent, and Timeline) used in my example above, because it is short and provides the basic information needed for leadership actions. In mapping out your timeline, envision several paths that you might take. Schedules and timelines must be determined step by step on a daily, weekly, and monthly basis. It is also necessary to set either monthly or bi-monthly timelines to determine 1) what objectives need to be addressed, 2) what research you will need to do for certain objectives, 3) what additional staff skills are need, and 4) when certain staff development trainings will need to be done to enable staff to accomplish the tasks in a timely manner.

The principal is responsible for monitoring all actions as well as overseeing who, what, how, when, and to what degree particular strategies are successful. The principal and the school leadership team will keep track of the planned tasks, objectives, and goals while remembering that the actions in other areas such as attendance, behavior, extra-curricular activities, and other school-day organizational elements will be going on at the same time.

Throughout the Action Phase, leadership coaching can be valuable one-to-one support for the principal's leadership actions. In addition to coaching the principal in the area of growth in personal dimensions, the coach can also conduct targeted observations of the organization's objectives. Feedback to the principal from these observations can be valuable content for the dialogue between the coach and the principal in determining further leadership strategies.

Action planning is a cyclical process. As reflected in the School Principal Change Model™, you can start again at the beginning based upon the evaluation results produced from the initial implementation.

Phase 5: Results

CHARACTERISTIC: TRANSFORMATION

"Great results require total transformation."
—F. Lovelady-Spain

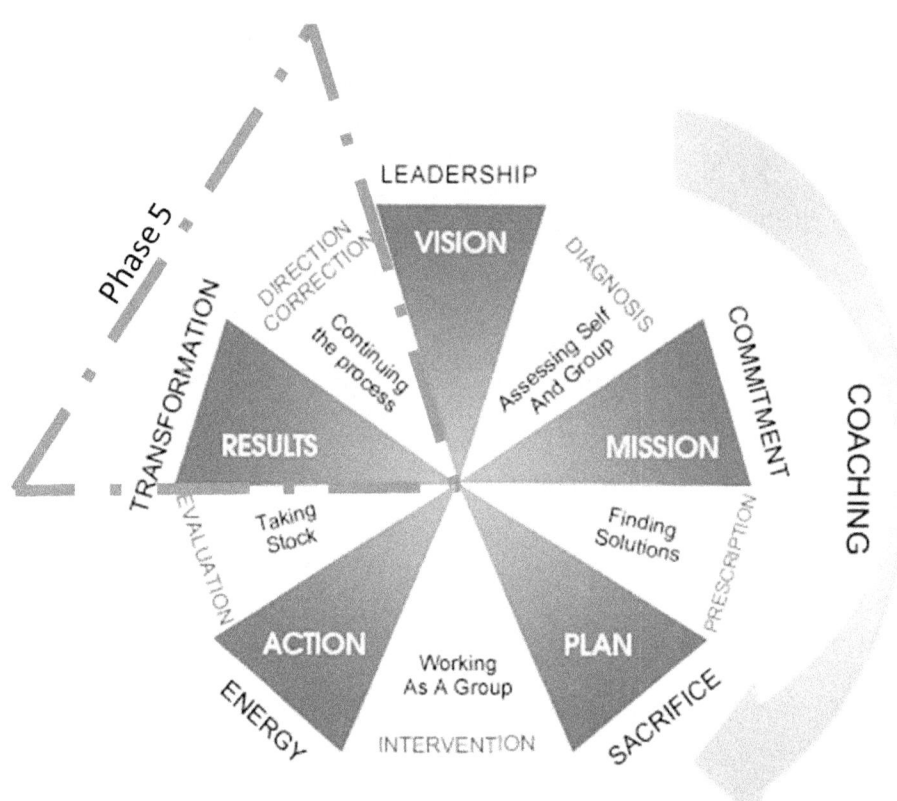

Phase 5 - *Results*, is the final phase of the School Principal Change Model™. This is the phase in which the principal and the school leadership team will evaluate the effect or results that interventions and collective actions are making/have made on the school program and the school environment. *Evaluation* is the systematic collection and analysis of data needed to make decisions. There are many reasons to conduct evaluations, including:

- To determine the effectiveness of the programs for participants
- To document that program objectives have been met

- To provide information about service delivery that will be useful to staff and shareholders
- To allow staff to make changes that improve program effectiveness

Evaluation can help a school nurture accountability as well as establish whether or not programs are making the difference that the school intended. Evaluation can help to ensure that project activities continue to reflect project plans and goals.

It is important that the school team create a detailed work plan for conducting the evaluation. In creating an evaluation program for the school, issues such as who will use the information, what questions are most important, what data and/or records will be examined, what analyses will be conducted, and how will the results be displayed and disseminated need to be answered to guide the design of an effective evaluation process. As stated earlier, evaluation should be systematic and conducted simultaneously with program implementation. *Taking Stock* or monitoring programs on a systematic basis can accomplish this.

If the evaluation of school programs produces the intended outcomes, then the school leadership team can celebrate. If, on the other hand, the findings do not produce the predicted outcomes, it is advisable for the principal and the school leadership team to 'Continue the Process,' beginning with the first step in the SPCM™ process. The second cycle should prove easier as it is expected that many of the milestones will be met and mistakes made the first time around will not be repeated. These two factors will combine to reduce the timeline the second time around. An example of an evaluation activity is included in Chapter 8: Tools, Techniques and Other Resources for your use and consideration.

It is critical to remember that the principal is the key person to lead change in the school and that principals can be more effective in leading change when they are supported. Leadership coaching is most successful when it focuses on those areas self-identified by the principal and are integrated into the entire improvement process throughout the implementation of the School Principal Change Model™. In this way, the coach and the principal work together to strengthen only those personal dimensions and competences required to successfully implement the change process.

Looking at results requires evaluating outcomes and making necessary direction corrections. The principal and the leadership team are responsible for conducting the evaluation, which can be a way of taking stock. Evaluation is most effective when it is built into the fabric of the educational program rather than added on after the fact.

Results are outcomes from a given set of behaviors. Staffs are more likely to use the results of the evaluation when they play a role in deciding what to examine, and are involved in conducting the evaluation and in the interpretation of the results.

The final outcome expected by implementing the School Principal Change Model™ is transformation. A school has transformed when the people within it think and act differently as a team. Schools and principals can transform themselves by making sure there is an organized set of clear and focused personal and school goals. These goals must be developed through collaboration that involves the entire team. Everyone in the organization must commit to accomplishing these goals. The climate in the school must be positive and productive, with a common vocabulary used to articulate student expectations and classroom strategies. Staff members must engage in problem-solving conversations, as a learning community, which promotes positive interactions. Doing all of these things on a collective and consistent basis within the school engenders focus on the school's mission and purpose. The results are transformational in both personal and school behaviors.

As principals, we are charged with making a difference in the lives of our children, our most precious resource. Marzano, Waters and McNulty (2005) state, "The need for truly educational leadership is great; the time for improving our schools is short; the opportunity to lead is ours; the knowledge needed is available; and the only thing left is to act." I remain convinced that, collectively, we can still make a great impact on student achievement in our nation's schools.

CHAPTER 5

The School Principal Change Model™ Combined
with Leadership Coaching: A Remedy

---

*"Coaching is a methodology that allows us to work with
change on a personal level, on an organizational level,
on a relationship level."*
—Henry Kimsey-House, Karen Kimsey-House, Phillip Sandahl

A New Approach for the
Ongoing Staff Development of Principals

In this chapter, I provide a rationale for leadership coaching as the right strategy through personal stories, a brief history of coaching, and several definitions of coaching. I also make some distinctions between coaching and other similar processes, establish how coaching works, and briefly discuss what I think it takes to make personal change and transformation.

In the School Principal Change Model™, the change process and the leadership coaching strategies are combined to offer onsite, site-specific and ongoing staff development to the entire school. The methodology used in the coaching process remains the same whether coaching the principal or the school team. However, the techniques and the focus will change. In coaching the principal, leadership and its attending elements are the focus; while in coaching the school as a group, collaboration and team-building are the focus. The collective goal is to produce changes in knowledge, understanding, behaviors and skills of the principal and the entire school, enabling them to make a greater impact on student outcomes.

THE RIGHT STRATEGY

> *"It is easy to acquire the content knowledge needed to lead schools. It is not so easy to change who we are to acquire the personal traits necessary for success."*
>
> —Karla Reiss

With the new call for effective leadership, it is essential to have an accompanying call for a new strategy. A strategy that offers immediate support and professional development for the principal that is "onsite, site-specific and ongoing."

To illustrate the importance of the right strategy, my own personal experience might serve as instructive. After several years, I was afforded the opportunity to compete for an education policy fellowship, a program of the George Washington University Institute for Educational Leadership. I applied, as did 2500 other hopefuls, and won a placement at the National Institute of Education, which at that time was the research arm of Congress. As part of the experience, I completed the Myers-Briggs Type Inventory. After careful analysis by the consultant, I was informed that I was classified as an INFJ, meaning that I fit the profile of an Introvert who is Intuitive, whose decisions are based on Feelings and Judgment.

The MBTI is designed to help an individual understand where they are on these dimensions, and offers insight into how best to listen, understand and communicate with other personality types. It is also useful in helping an individual realize that different styles of communication can be a block to performance or can, with understanding, enhance interpersonal interactions and team efforts.

I returned from my fellowship after a year, and eventually returned to the school site. As part of our professional development, my district took the administrative staff on a retreat. Most of the retreat agenda was focused on strategic planning for the district. However, as an exercise, we were given the Myers-Briggs Type Inventory. I was quite anxious to find out if I would score the same way on the west coast as I did on the east coast. I was sure that it would not be the same because of my suspicions regarding its validity. To my great surprise, I was still classified as an INFJ.

Time passed and in conversation with my daughter, I complained that people did not understand me and I was often viewed as combative. I told her of my deep convictions about education and that I was not afraid to express these convictions. I said that my evaluations were always outstanding, but that I still felt tension coming from my staff as well as my supervisors. She listened and in her quiet, gentle, but firm way, pointed out that the tone of my voice interfered with the words I was saying; therefore, thenonverbal message was what was being heard. She described my voice as very strong. She also pointed out that I make grand and sudden movements with my hands as I speak. She continued to explain that many people may be threatened by this combination. What a revelation!

In retrospect, I realized that I had my first coaching experience regarding my leadership behaviors. I could now bring some meaning to the Myers-Briggs results that I had taken on two separate occasions some years before. With deeper explanation and follow-up by the consultant or the district personnel department, this information could have been of great value to me earlier in my career. It could have helped me understand and adjust the behaviors that were interfering with my ability to communicate more clearly.

After that conversation, instead of doubting the accuracy of her advice, I began to monitor my voice and my body movements. I spoke more softly and limited my hand gestures. I became an astute observer of myself. Over time, I began to notice a change in the way in which staff members and supervisors related to me. Staff began to approach me more often and in a more relaxed manner. I became a trusted confidant for many of them. In fact, I still get calls from many of my former teachers.

Realizing that the system was not organized to provide me with the follow-up support that I needed, I adopted the adage, "If it is going to be, it is up to me." I carefully chose workshops and conferences to attend, ones that offered more coaching and practice experiences. Over time, these choices have proven beneficial. I began applying the insights gained to all areas and dimensions of my life and leadership. You might say I became my own curriculum, meaning that I already knew what I needed to know to resolve my problems; I only had to be willing to ask myself the questions, admit my shortcomings, and make a plan to change.

I remain grateful to my daughter for the coaching insight that she awakened within me. It worked for me because I became stronger and more introspective. It shifted my thinking and changed my life.

Motivated by my change journey, I wanted to write this book and document the lessons I have learned so that no other principal will have to wait as long to get the coaching support and professional development they need and deserve.

The School Principal Change Model™ employs two coaching strategies. The first coaching strategy is facilitated by the Expert School Change Coach (ESCC), who works with the entire school team so the school becomes an effective learning institution. The ESCC owns the relationship with the school and customizes, trains, and supports the implementation of all five phases of the SPCM™.

The second coaching process is facilitated by the Certified Leadership Coach (CLC), who works almost exclusively with the principal in private sessions. The topic of these sessions can include personal development goals that the principal self-selects, as well as other issues that are discovered in the leadership assessment process. These issues may include leadership skills and competencies, areas of personal productivity, team effectiveness skills and building staff morale, to name a few. The three primary goals of the Expert School Change Coach (ESCC) and the Certified Leadership Coach (CLC) are:

1. To coach the principal and the school team to access what they already know and declare it as valuable

2. To coach the principal and the school team to unleash personal and team potential

3. To coach the principal and the school team to identify areas of need, develop personal and team action plans, and take steps to eliminate identified deficiencies.

The SPCM™ is a guide for the principal and the school team to implement continuous improvement, step by step. The process is designed to initiate the right actions in an orderly manner at the right time. It can be used by the principal as a leadership tool and by the leadership team for school improvement actions. It can also be used by curriculum focus groups or by the entire school community for strategic planning, implementation, progress monitoring and evaluation.

The leadership coaches use carefully selected assessment instruments to create profiles for the principal and the school team. Appropriate coaching techniques are selected and implemented based on the assessment analysis. The leadership coaches observe and provide feedback to the principal and the school team. By using the coaching methodology and appropriate techniques, the leadership coaches address the principal's leadership needs and/or the team's organizational needs.

I believe that permanent change and transformation occur as a result to two things: an effective change process, and an accompanying effective staff development program. The systematic combination of these two functions produces transformation.

To test the efficacy of the SPCM™, I compared my model to the findings from a study outlined in a Southwest Educational Development Laboratory's (SEDL) journal. The issue was about change, and the article was titled "Staff Development and Change Process: Cut from the Same Cloth." (SEDL Letter, 1994). It stated that the study involved several school districts, including several principals and their campus-based and central office-based colleagues. The design combined a staff development model with a change process model in order to observe the implications for using staff development as the process for change. In the multi-district study, five functional categories of interventions necessary when intervening for change were identified and observed in each district. The five functional categories are the same as the findings outlined by Hall and Hord, (1987), Hord (1992) and Hord, Rutherford, Huling-Austin, and Hall (1987). These functional categories included the following:

1. Articulating a vision of the change and its attendant goals and expectations

2. Planning, providing resources, and making organizational arrangements

3. Training and development of skills necessary for change

4. Monitoring and evaluation of the change process

5. Consultation, reinforcement, and other data-based interventions

Of the five functional categories of interventions for change, the four most frequent categories collected included organizational arrangements, training and development, monitoring and evaluation, consultation and reinforcement. These categories accounted for 84% - 96% of the interventions observed and documented.

Also included in the study were findings by Hord (1992), Boyd (1992), and Mendez-Morse (1992), who found that leaders of change use specific strategies. These researchers observed that context factors support change and that "change leaders" possess certain characteristics. Hence, when the principals and the principals' facilitators provided a number of the interventions to the faculties, there was a strong correlation with implementation success.

The Joyce and Showers (1980) model of staff development was used to train the staff in the various interventions. In the instances in which school faculty received all five components of the staff development model (theory, demonstration, practice, feedback and coaching), combined with an increased number of the change interventions, they experienced successful transfer of skills into classroom practice.

In conclusion, the School Principal Change Model™ is firmly rooted in the research on effective change strategies and effective staff development techniques. I remain committed to leadership coaching as the "bridging strategy" that brings theory and practice together.

BRIEF HISTORY OF COACHING

Coaching as a discipline is new, but the act of coaching is not. Coaching has been around for a very long time. Elements of coaching have been used from the earliest of times. More recently, between the late 1930s and the late 1960s, coaching literature focused on internal coaching in organizations, with managers or supervisors acting as coaches to their staff. Gorby (1937) detailed how older employees were trained to coach new employees. Bigelow (1938), in another publication, discusses the benefits of sales coaching. In 1958, Mold reported on the benefits of manager-as-coach. During the 1960s, life skills coaching began in New York as part of education program development, and Mahler (1964) observed the difficulty in getting managers to be effective coaches. In 1967, Gershman produced his doctoral research thesis on how supervisors were trained to be successful coaches to improve employees' attitudes and job performance. The roots of the terms 'executive coaching' and 'business coaching' became well known in the leadership development program movement of the 1980s. Different aspects of coaching are used in today's workplace in the form of guiding, mentoring, and questioning.

LEADERSHIP COACHING DEFINED: WHAT COACHING IS

The way in which we describe coaching today is new. It is a fusion of the three types of coaching-life skills, business, and executive. Since the 1930s, a clearer definition of leadership coaching has emerged and a more efficient process has been designed.

In searching for a working definition for leadership coaching as advanced in this book, I chose the comprehensive description provided by Zeus & Skiffington (2002) as the guiding principles for the coaching process I employ. They state and I agree that:

- "*Coaching is essentially a conversation*—a dialogue between a coach and a [principal]—within a productive, results-oriented context. Coaching involves helping individuals *access what they know*. They may never have asked themselves the questions, but they have the answers. A coach assists, supports and encourages the individuals to find these answers.

- *"Coaching is about learning*—yet a coach is not a teacher and does not necessarily know how to do things better than the principal. A coach can observe patterns, set the stage for new actions and then work with the individual to put these new, more successful actions into place. Coaching involves learning. Through various coaching techniques such as listening, reflecting, asking questions and providing information, principals become self-correcting (they learn how to correct their behavior themselves) and self-generating (they generate their own questions and answers).

- *"Coaching is more about asking the right questions than providing answers.* A coach engages in a collaborative alliance with the individual to establish and clarify purpose and goals, and to develop a plan of action to achieve these goals."

They further state that *"Coaching is about change and transformation—the ability to recognize and alter non-productive behaviors; about reinventing oneself—*creating new stories, new identities and new futures. It recognizes that the self is not a fixed entity, but is fluid and always in a state of becoming. *Coaching is a journey where the journey is as important as the destination.* Coaching proposes a conduit for analysis, reflection and action that eventually empower people to achieve success in one or more areas of their life or work."

The following are additional definitions that clarify what leadership coaching is:

The Coaching Network compiled the following definitions:

Other Definitions

- "Coaching is the art and practice of guiding a person or group from where they are toward the greater competence and fulfillment that they desire." Gary Collins

- "Coaching is a dialogue, not a monologue." Joseph Umidi

- "Coaching is like having a personal trainer for every area of your life."

They also collected the following statements about coaches, personal change, and the distinction between mentoring and coaching:

- "Coaches are change experts who help leaders take responsibility and act to maximize their own potential."

- "Sustainable personal change and organizational transformation always honors the unique design, desires, dreams and destiny of its leaders." Joseph Umidi

- "Mentoring is imparting to you what God has given to me. Coaching is drawing out of you what God has put in you." Dale Stoll

WHAT COACHING IS NOT

It is important to make a distinction between what coaching is and what coaching is not, because many of the processes appear to be the same. I find in the work of Zeus and Skiffington (2002) clear definitions of coaching and comprehensible comparisons of the similarities and differences for each of the techniques:

- *Coaching is NOT mentoring.* Mentoring is a passing on of knowledge and experience through a hierarchical relationship between an experienced senior to an inexperienced junior. Coaching is a collaboration that empowers the individual to discover what he or she already knows.

- *Coaching is NOT consulting.* Coaching is not an expert model of consulting. The coach facilitates a process of reflection and action. A coach also stays with the principal to help implement the new skills, changes and goals in order to make sure they happen.

- *Coaching is NOT therapy.* Coaches do not work on "issues" or get into the past or deal much with understanding human behaviors. Coaches leave that up to the principal to figure out while the coach helps them move forward and set personal and professional goals, goals that will give them the life they really want.

- *Coaching is NOT training.* Most training programs have fixed predetermined scripts, and no support mechanism is put in place. Coaching provides individualized follow-up and feedback designed to allow the skills to be put into practice.

- *Coaching is NOT counseling.* Counseling is about finding the causes behind a particular problem or behavior. Considerable time is spent on why a given set of ideals are not met. Coaching is about emphasizing strengths and successes and building on those to create new skills and competencies.

- *Coaching is NOT sports.* Coaching includes several principles from sports coaching, like teamwork, going for the goal and being your best. But unlike sports coaching, most professional coaching is not competitive or win/lose-based. Coaches strengthen the principal's skills versus helping them beat someone else. It is as Steve Covey states, "win/win or no deal."

Of all of the processes covered above, coaching and mentoring share the most similarities. They both enable the principal to achieve their full potential. In summing up this section, I have combined the common attributes offered by the research on coaching and mentoring. The following reflects the commonalities.

COMMON ATTRIBUTES OF COACHING AND MENTORING

- Facilitate the exploration of needs, motivations, desires, skills and thought processes to assist the principal in making real, lasting change.

- Use questioning techniques to facilitate principal's thought processes in order to identify solutions and actions rather than take a wholly directive approach

- Support the principal in setting appropriate goals and methods of assessing progress in relation to these goals

- Observe, listen and ask questions to understand the principal's situation

- Creatively apply tools and techniques which may include one-to-one training, facilitating, counseling and networking

- Encourage a commitment to action and the development of lasting personal growth and change

- Maintain unconditional positive regard for the principal, which means that the coach is at all times supportive and non-judgmental of the individual, their views, lifestyle and aspirations

- Ensure that principals develop personal competencies and do not develop unhealthy dependencies on the coaching or mentoring relationship

- Evaluate the outcomes of the process, using objective measures wherever possible to ensure the relationship is successful and the principal is achieving his or her personal goals
- Encourage principals to continually improve competencies and to develop new developmental alliances where necessary to achieve their goals
- Work within their area of personal competence
- Possess qualifications and experience in the areas that skill-transfer coaching is offered
- Manage the relationship to ensure the principal receives the appropriate level of service, and the sessions are neither too short nor too long.

In summary, it is of critical importance to remember that coaching is different from mentoring because coaching assumes the principal knows the school better than anyone from the outside. The coaching strategy will assist the principal to arrive at, and be committed to, sensible, workable solutions. The principal owns the strategies for change because they have not been imposed from outside or above.

HOW COACHING WORKS

The coach and principal must commit to a trusting, mutually respectful climate. Both must give and receive honest feedback. The coach must have a genuine commitment to the needs of the principal and should guide, support and encourage learning.

Reiss (2007) depicts the coaching relationship best. In the table on the next page, she gives a graphic representation of this relationship and shows the primary roles required by each member of the coaching process. Note that confidentiality and dialogue are the key components in this adult learning paradigm:

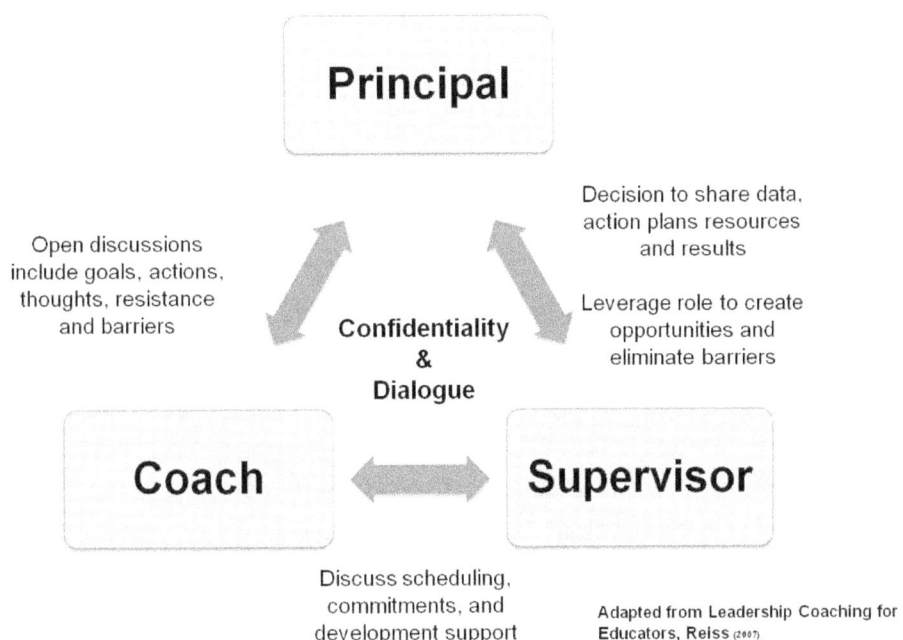

Coaching is about developing and enhancing strengths. The coach uses appropriate techniques designed to maximize what the principal already knows. All of the experiences, past and present, are used as resources by the coach to enhance learning. It is important that the coach accepts how the principal prefers to learn and builds the successes and failures into the coaching experience. The major role of the coach is to provide the opportunity for the principal to assess and clarify his or her needs in the present circumstances.

The coaching process is always about the real-time issues that the principal faces on a daily basis. The coach's role is to ensure that the principal has opportunities to apply what is discussed and learned in the coaching sessions. In the School Principal Change Model™, this is done by assigning homework to the principal and the entire staff. By implementing the activities assigned, the school team is actually applying the strategies that lead to improvement and change. During the time between coach visits, the coach consults with the principal via phone, Skype, and/or the interactive website. This strategy allows the coach to monitor and give (and receive) feedback on the practice of the new or enhanced skills and capabilities. This process is built to begin with coaching the principal, who then applies the personal skills and competencies into leading the school through a systematic change process.

HOW COACHING IS INITIATED

More often than not, school organizations have not previously implemented a leadership coaching program for principals in their districts. The following discussion will give you an idea of how the leadership coaching process is initiated and launched within a district and school context. Leadership coaching is organized into a set of four modules.

The initial visit with the district administration is designated Module I. It is designed to establish a context in which coaching can be successful. Generally building on the findings of Zeus and Skiffington cited above, the organization has some ideas of individuals that they wish to recommend for coaching services. Therefore, it is important for the coach to meet with the organization's leaders to ascertain: 1) the particular challenges they perceive the principal as having in general; 2) the reason the coaching process was chosen over other processes; 3) the reason a particular principal was chosen; 4) the amount of information this principal knows about coaching, and 5) whether or not the principal volunteered or was assigned a coach. Once these issues are adequately addressed, the coach is ready to establish the personal and leadership competencies necessary for the principal's success. Coaches combine the leadership assessments with the competencies required by a particular state for certification and together with the principal build an action plan based on the combined results.

Having established the context for the coaching role in a particular district, the next task is to establish the logistics of intervention. The coach begins this task by gathering answers to such questions as: Will the coaches meet with the principal prior to the first formal session? Will all sessions be on-site or a combination of on-site/off-site? Will some sessions occur by phone or email or on-line interactive? How often will the sessions be held? What is the initial time frame for the coaching intervention? What are the contractual agreements? Are there sufficient resources to support the coaching program? Additional questions are formed and addressed as deemed appropriate.

Module II is the first formal coaching session with the principal. This task involves some form of assessment. Principals should be informed that the assessment is an efficient way of gathering data, the results of which can benefit both the coach and the principal in the coaching process. It is also important that the coach reassures and discusses with the principal the strict protocol that will be kept in the use of data derived from the assessments. Also, that all personal assessment data will be strictly confidential and that any data that the coach is required to share with the administration is revealed with principal sign-off. The principal should know that the assessment data will be directly related to what can be used in the coaching intervention and for goal-setting. In this session, it is important that the coach listens and provides answers that will advance the process.

There are a number of assessment instruments that are frequently used to measure various dimensions. Experts in the field recommend that the best assessments are ones that: 1) are specific to the issues being addressed; 2) are structured as question-and-answer interviews; 3) are no longer than an hour in length; 4) contain no right or wrong answers, and 5) the leader's self-ratings are held confidential. The sole purpose of the interview is to gather information that can inform the coaching intervention.

Module III involves the coach's giving feedback from the assessment. It is important that the feedback is given in a manner to engender acceptance and commitment to change. Here, in collaboration with the principal, commitment to broad goals for both the principal and coach can be agreed upon. In addition to the broader goals, other issues involving the principal as leader of the change process are identified to be addressed in future sessions.

Module IV constitutes the ongoing coaching sessions and depends on the period of time allocated to the coaching intervention. These sessions will examine, recognize and challenge any self-limiting beliefs; examine values, vision and purpose; establish goals; develop action plans, and follow-up. When the coaching modules are completed, the coach can switch to a mentoring role and offer opinions and suggestions regarding strategies to coaching the principal and the leadership team through the systemic change process. This transition is recommended only if the coach has the proper credentials and experience as a school principal.

It is important that all of the following elements are adhered to if leadership coaching for principals is to be successful:

1. Coaching is used as the primary strategy for increasing the leadership effectiveness of principals

2. On-site, site-specific and ongoing coaching is delivered by an experienced coach who may also be a mentor principal

3. 'Cognitive coaching' is used to support principals as they transfer new knowledge and skills into practice at their worksites

4. Coaching is designed to help principals become more effective learners

5. Coaching is supported with adequate resources (time, money, governance and policy)

Leadership coaching holds promise for improving the effectiveness of principals in our schools. Now is the time for educational policymakers and leaders to move forward to integrate leadership coaching for principals into the overall strategy for leadership development, succession planning, and performance management. Research has confirmed that coaching is the professional development differentiator.

ADULT LEARNING ASSUMPTIONS IN COACHING PROCESS

Coaching is a learning process and, as such, reflects the principles put forth by leading researchers in the field of adult learning. One such researcher is Malcolm Knowles. In his book, *The Modern Practice of Adult Education* (1980), he makes five assumptions about adult learning. He states that as people mature:

- their self-concept is no longer dependent on others but becomes more self-directed

- their accumulated knowledge becomes a resource for learning

- they have a great need and become more willing to learn when it will help them deal with real-life issues

- they want to be able to apply the knowledge and skills they learn now, so that they can live more effectively in the future

- their motivation to learn becomes internal

Professional development programs can be of maximum value when they build these adult learning assumptions into their coaching models. In the next list, Skiffington and Zeus (2002) show how the coaching process addresses these assumptions:

- a suitably qualified and experienced coach is identified, and agreed to, by the principal
- the coach gathers general background information about the school and principal
- the coach and principal meet in a one-on-one, confidential setting
- the coach and principal agree on an issue for discussion and exploration; for example, a phase in the School Principal Change Model™, a staff problem, a resource matter, or a curriculum priority
- the coach assists the principal to set a goal(s) relevant to the issue
- a wide range of options are discussed, then discarded or adopted (an experienced principal as coach can be useful here in mentoring and gently making suggestions)
- the principal arrives at solutions and strategies with careful and subtle assistance from the coach (once again, an experienced principal as coach can be useful here)
- the principal develops and commits to an action plan
- a time frame is set (and must be strictly adhered to)
- a number of sessions is agreed upon and is reached on the principal providing feedback to the coach and the coach providing support and advice to the principal
- progressive contact is made on-site, preferably, and by telephone and email
- A session is organized at the end of the agreed time frame to assess progress toward the stated goal(s).

CHAPTER 6

Review of the Relevant Research

---

*"You cannot teach a man anything. You can only
help him discover it within himself."*
—Galileo

Best Practices for Effective Leadership and Coaching

Education is entirely about change – about drawing things out of people and creating the generations of the future. Effective change is inalienably about learning – figuring out the best way forward for the greatest good (Fullan, 2009). My philosophy regarding leadership coaching for principals is congruent with these ideas. Leadership coaching is about learning. "Through various coaching techniques such as listening, reflecting, asking questions and providing information, [the principal] becomes self-correcting (they learn how to correct their behavior themselves) and self-generating (they generate their own questions and answers)." (Zeus & Skiffington, 2002).

ABOUT EFFECTIVE LEADERSHIP

"A great leader's courage to fulfill his [her] vision comes from passion, not position."

—John Maxwell

Effective leaders convey a vision and, through their example, expand others' view of what is possible. They set high expectations, create a strong sense of community, and get results. Leaders accomplish this both by what they do, as well as by who they are. In terms of tasks, good leaders "enhance the skills and knowledge of the people in the organization, create a common culture of expectations around the use of those skills and knowledge, hold the various pieces of the organization together in a productive relationship with each other, and hold individuals accountable for their contributions to the collective results." (Elmore, 2000).

Effective leaders act, not only because their jobs mandate it, but also because their own belief system requires it. Their life purpose, values and assumptions drive their life choices. Everything they do is consistent with their values. As a result, they motivate and inspire others to want to be like them.

It is commonly believed, and I agree, that the leadership of any organization is fundamental to the success of that institution. This belief is correspondingly true for educational institutions, especially schools. To illustrate this belief, I have compiled the following list of research findings that identify several of the factors that correlate to leadership in a school building:

---

1. Clear mission and goals (Bamburg & Andrews, 1990; Duke, 1982).
2. The overall climate of the school and the climate in individual classrooms (Brookover & Lezotte, 1979; Griffith, 2000; Villani, 1996).
3. The attitudes of teachers (Brookover & Lezotte, 1979; Oakes, 1989; Purkey & Smith, 1983; Rutter, Maughan, Mortimore, Ouston, & Smith, 1979).

4. The classroom practices of teachers (Brookover et al., 1978; Brookover & Lezotte, 1979; McDill, Rigsby, & Meyers, 1969; Miller & Sayre, 1986).

5. The organization of curriculum and instruction (Bossert, Dwyer, Rowan, & Lee, 1982; Cohen & Miller, 1980; Eberts & Stone, 1988; Glasman & Biniaminov, 1981; Oakes, 1989)

6. Students' opportunity to learn (Duke & Canady, 1991; Murphy & Hallinger, 1989).

———————□ □ □———————

The degree that these factors are systematically and effectively addressed in schools is the degree to which the schools will experience success. Numerous reforms in education have been implemented in an attempt to address these schooling factors. The staff development programs designed to help schools deliver these reforms, for the most part, have been traditional in their approach. Some of the methods most commonly used include: participation on district task forces, leadership teams, school improvement teams, school reform task forces, workshops, seminars and conferences.

These methods also include the use of mentors, peer groups, consultants, pre-service and in-service trainings. Many school leaders also return to colleges and universities to obtain advanced degrees and certifications. Some even pursue speaking opportunities at workshops and conferences.

While beneficial, these trainings and activities are limited. They do not provide the follow-up support needed for school leaders to transfer the learning to their day-to-day behaviors and actions. In many instances, there is marginal or minimum system responsibility to monitor and ensure that the intended goals for the trainings and activities are translated into practice.

The business sector and nonprofit sector have contributed tremendously to the research on effective leadership. They have been using the executive coaching model, as a strategy to increase performance of its top executives, for a number of years with documented successes. Reuters, in a press release, announced a study titled, "Trends in Executive Coaching: New Research Reveals Emerging Best Practice." (Trends in Executive Coaching, 2008). This study of nearly 500 business and human capital leaders found that:

- the demand for executive coaching services is growing due to increased credibility
- executive coaching has demonstrated an impact on the enterprise.

The key findings of this study include:

---

1. Organizations are benefiting from a high return on investment (ROI) for executive coaching

2. More than three-quarters of enterprise executives view executive coaching as credible and valuable

3. Investment in coaching is on the rise as organizations strive to build pipelines of talent

4. Coaching is viewed as very positive and demonstrates an organization's commitment to the employee's success in both current and future roles

5. When executives were asked to rank the top circumstances where executive coaching has the greatest impact, the top three greatest opportunities they cited were:

   - Developing "high potential" candidates for succession planning (29%)

   - Helping a capable executive achieve a higher level of performance (28%)

   - Addressing derailing behaviors (22%)

Another study (Bradley, et al., 2006), comprised of 24 executive directors of nonprofits who received 40 hours of one-on-one coaching over the course of a year, found that coaching provided greater confidence in executing leadership, improved ability to communicate and advance the organization's vision, increased productivity, strengthened staff management skills, and improved relationships between staff and board members.

In a survey conducted by MetrixGlobal (2001) of 4000+ corporations on their involvement with corporate coaching, the primary benefits of coaching reported are (in order):

1. Improved individual performance

2. Bottom-line results (including profits)

3. Client service and competitiveness

4. Development of people for the next level, including confidence-raising, skills and self-empowerment, goal achievement, relationship improvements, and retention

A study of 100 executives in the private sector who received coaching reported that the average return on investment (ROI) of their coaching was 5.7 times the cost of the coaching (a 570% ROI). In another study, 43 executive of Fortune 500 companies found that coaching produced a 529% return on investment. When the financial benefits from employee retention were included, the ROI for the Fortune 500 study was 788%.

There is also some evidence from school districts in the United States and other countries such as Canada, which provide some important implications for coaching as a strategy for staff development. One formal study (Marzano, et al., 2005) conducted in British Columbia involved 18 principals, vice principals, and district office administrators. The study found that "coaching resulted in the participants gaining new skills; taking different approaches in their jobs; increasing their [sense of] wellbeing; gaining better balance, and feeling supported, all results which [are likely to] increase the effectiveness of the school district's leaders and will likely retain them as leaders."

SELECTED MODELS AND PROGRAMS

In researching change and looking for a better way forward, I have reviewed several programs' models that offer coaching and mentoring as the primary approach to professional development. They are offered in somewhat different formats, such as workshops, seminars, modules, on-line and one-to-one coaching at the school sites. These programs are located at varying levels of the education strata: departments of education, colleges and universities, research laboratories, professional organizations, districts and schools. I have, with minor edits, used the descriptions provided by the entities. In a few cases, I have summarized the programs as they did not provide extensive information, but do contain the coaching or mentoring aspect which is the crucial thread linking all the programs. I selected these programs because, for the most part, they met the Joyce and Showers criteria.

THE MICHIGAN PRINCIPALS FELLOWSHIP AND COACHES INSTITUTE

Michigan State University

The Michigan Principals Fellowship (MPF) is a research-based approach to school improvement that provides principals and their instructional leadership teams with essential knowledge, skills, experiences and support that enable them to lead systematic instructional improvement and increase student achievement.

This three-year program has been developed as a central component of the Statewide System of Support (SSOS), the Michigan Department of Education's strategy for supporting high-poverty, low-performing schools. MPF is a program within the College of Education at Michigan State University.

The organization of the Fellowship work ensures that principals and teachers have the fundamentals to begin and sustain instructional improvement in their schools as well as the practical tools and skills to identify which changes will translate into significant gains in student achievement.

Participants in the Michigan Principals Fellowship are strongly encouraged to include a school improvement (leadership) coach as part of their reform plan and budget. Just as principals are the key mechanism for improving instructional quality in schools, leadership coaches are the key mechanism for providing on-site support that builds the capacity of school leadership teams.

Specifically, the role of a leadership coach is to increase the capacity of school leaders to develop and exercise skills and practices related to visionary, instructional and operational leadership, as well as the cross-cutting skills needed to exercise leadership in all areas. For this reason, schools are strongly encouraged to include a leadership coach in their school improvement grant proposals and budgets.

THE KENTUCKY COHESIVE LEADERSHIP SYSTEM (KyCLS)

Kentucky Department of Education

Kentucky, along with seven other states, piloted a coaching model, Kentucky Cohesive Leadership System (KyCLS), with beginning principals and some experienced ones. KyCLS grew out of a study conducted by the Wallace Foundation Leaderships Issues Group: Assessing Leadership Effectiveness.

The Leadership Performance Worksheet, developed by the Issues Group, helps new principals identify, organize around and effectively lead instructional improvement in their schools. The Worksheet is composed of 37 core behaviors that are organized into nine leadership dimensions. This list was created from a review and synthesis of principal leadership audit protocols and assessments designed by the New York City Leadership Academy, the states of Delaware and Kentucky, and the Wallace Foundation Driver Behaviors. Each behavior was selected for:

- Its ability to address the expected scope of new principals' critical job demands
- Its generalizability to a wide variety of state performance standards for principals
- Its usefulness to new principals of different experience levels

This tool is specifically designed to assist principal development of the leadership skills and behaviors to meet the goals of leading and improving schools instructionally. Each principal is assigned a Leadership Development Coach as a collaborative effort of the KyCLS and KDE SAM (Kentucky, Delaware School Administration Manager) Project, and the Kentucky Leadership Academy.

Additionally, Kentucky has developed the "cohesive leadership system" that is a system-wide approach to enhancing leadership. While complicated and challenging, it offers a pathway for moving the collective thinking among state and district policy-makers away from isolated or uncoordinated efforts on single elements of leadership improvement. It holds considerable potential to speed up and make more permanent the advances being made in developing leadership that benefits the learning of all students, using a more system-wide, coordinated approach to state, district and school level policies and practice. As I observed in my introduction, this is the ideal structural change needed to make the greatest impact on school and student outcomes.

The pillars of a cohesive system, if successfully implemented and sustained, can result in states and districts working more collaboratively so that:

- State and district leadership standards are well-aligned and based on a widely accepted definition of what successful leadership is and how leaders actually need to behave in order to achieve it
- Leadership training is closely tied to standards and highly responsive to the job conditions, needs and learning goals of districts
- Continuing professional development opportunities for leaders are linked to learning goals, and principals have many opportunities to share challenges, successes and effective practices

- Leadership is shared and distributed rather than resting with single leaders
- Decision-making is fact-based, appropriate data related to learning goals are gathered by states and districts, and leaders are well-trained in their use
- Leaders have the necessary authority to allocate the people, time and money to meet student learning needs; and incentives are geared to focus leaders' performance on successful practice and encourage high-quality principals to work in districts and schools that most need them

To summarize, a cohesive leadership system can result in many more districts developing a sufficient pipeline of well-prepared future leaders rather than relying on a search for superheroes. It could mean better coordinated state and district policies that provide the conditions and incentives for leaders to succeed, rather than the status quo in which leaders must try, usually in vain, to beat an unsupportive system. In a more cohesive system, successes in improving teaching and learning could more readily spread to entire schools, districts and states through careful documentation, rather than remaining hidden, isolated and unproven in single classrooms. And because they are fact-based and widely shared, effective ideas about teaching and learning would be likelier to survive transitions in school or district leadership.

DEPARTMENT OF EDUCATION AND EARLY CHILDHOOD DEVELOPMENT

Victoria, British Columbia

Professional Coaching for Principals is a leadership development program offered by the Victoria Department of Education for emerging leaders, aspiring leaders, principals, early childhood education support staff, postgraduates, teams and networks, coaches and mentoring. Modules offered include Literacy Coaching, Numeracy Coaching and Mentoring Matters.

Through working with a skilled professional coach, principals, leadership teams and collegiate groups build their leadership capacity. The program is designed to challenge principals to think of new ways to enhance their leadership capacities and their role as effective leaders of school improvement. Coaching supports school leaders to develop their sense of efficacy as individuals and as leaders. The key role of the coach is to help principals gain clarity about themselves. Coaching assists school leaders to grasp their own potential and to identify areas of further capability development.

LEADERSHIP COACHING

Seattle University College of Education

The College of Education at Seattle University created a model program to assist graduates from the Education Administration Program transition into their beginning roles as principals. The program for new principals is the first graduate education program in the Northwest to provide structured support for new administrators through leadership coaching and ongoing professional development certification. Funded by Washington Mutual, Stuart Foundation and J. P. Morgan Chase, the program offers coach training for experienced school administrators. The two components are:

- Coaching support for graduates of Seattle University's Educational Administration Program who become assistant principals, principals, and program administrators (coaching support for other new administrators from participating school districts is also provided)

- Training for leadership coaches for new administrators from Seattle University and participating school districts

Coaches provide four to six hours a month of one-to-one, on-site leadership coaching to new administrators. These sessions include feedback for the new administrator on classroom observations, post-observations, post-observation conferences, and parent and faculty meetings. They also provide the new administrator opportunities to problem-solve in a confidential, supportive environment. Leadership coaches are retired administrators who are committed to developing exceptional leaders, who want to make a difference, and who see themselves as change agents in pursuit of excellence for students. Leadership coaches are required to participate in a three-day workshop in the summer and four follow-up sessions throughout the school year. The training helps the leadership coach learn strategies and skills such as:

- Trust-building
- Listening
- Questioning
- Problem-solving

Program evaluations are also provided to school district administrators.

ALASKA STATEWIDE MENTOR PROJECT

The Alaska Statewide Mentor Project is a principal coaching program for new school principals. The goal is to increase the retention rate of principals and give them skills to be effective instructional leaders. The coaches are retired administrators with demonstrated success as instructional leaders and who have experience in many educational settings. The coaches are trained in workshops and seminars in instructional leadership, school management, human resources and student services.

NYC LEADERSHIP ACADEMY

The NYC Leadership Academy offers coaching programs for new and experienced principals. The program is deeply connected to day-to-day work as a school leader and is designed to help school leaders create and sustain school improvement that maximizes student learning. At the time of this writing, more than 375 new and experienced New York City principals chose to participate in the coaching programs.

The coaches are recently retired principals and superintendents current with NYC-DOE accountability tools, leadership competencies and other reform initiatives, and trained in the Facilitative, Competency-based (FCB) coaching methodology. As a confidential thought partner, the coach creates a trusting, collaborative environment, enabling school leaders to engage in critical and targeted reflection on their practice as an instructional leader. The coaches know and understand the NYC-DOE, its latest initiatives and regulations, budgetary and organizational matters, and when and where to get help. All Leadership Academy coaching is aligned to NYC School Leadership Competencies and is offered in service plans that school leaders choose.

The day-to-day work provides the context, and school leaders select the service plan that meets their needs. The coach schedules sessions and activities based on the school leaders' calendar and priorities, delivering the majority of coaching services in school settings.

REGION 10 EDUCATION SERVICE CENTER

Richardson, Texas

The Education Service Center provides participants with a unique program of one-to-one coaching sessions with a trained professional coach. Principals explore the intricacies of being successful within the context of the day-to-day challenges of their current positions.

Coaching enhances the professional skills and knowledge for maximum success by providing support and collaboration in a sustained learning environment to make effective campus principals even better. The program is for a principal's professional growth; it is not a tool to address or correct poor performance and is not an intervention for principals in need of improvement. The coaching offers 15 telephone sessions, with the first and last sessions in-person and off-site.

INSIGHTS2IMPROVEMENT, INC

Professional Development Program Management (PDPM)

The team of educational experts at Insights2Improvement, Inc. partners with districts and schools to effectively manage professional budgets. PDPM supports leadership retreats, strategies, planning days, professional development summits, superintendent conferences as well as school leadership coaching and development. Tightened budgets are making it tougher for districts of all sizes to provide the professional development needed, and districts may not have a designated professional development person with expertise in this area. Insights2Improvement provides a highly structured and data-driven coaching action experience for district leaders, principals, assistant principals, teacher leaders, and instructional coaches.

―――――――――――――― □ □ □ ――――――――――――

This literature search is by no means intended to be exhaustive. I chose to highlight these programs because they offered, in many ways, the components found by Bruce Joyce and Beverly Showers to be most effective in staff development programs. In their book *Student Achievement through Staff Development*, Joyce and Showers (2002) discuss a comprehensive staff development system to support teaching and learning. They suggest that there is a difference between training models which simply raise awareness and training models that change behavior. They advocate coaching as an essential ingredient in using knowledge to change practice.

CHAPTER 7

Conclusion

―▬◆▬―

"The best way to predict the future is to invent it now."
—Art Costa

The success of our nation depends on an educated workforce. As competition for jobs goes global, it is imperative that we arm our children with a quality education so they can effectively compete in the world economy. Our education system is governed by guidelines enacted at the federal level; however, the site principal, the teachers and the students must be at the top of the local, state and national agendas. Without proper alignment of national education policy with funding and implementation at the district and local levels, the needs of the principals who lead our schools, the teachers who deliver instruction to our students, and the needs of our students who learn will not be met. Every policy decision and resource allocation must directly support the leadership, teaching and learning process. Hoy and Hoy (2006) state that, "Schools are about teaching and learning; all other activities are secondary to these basic goals."

Education is a stimulating and demanding profession. We need a model to provide ongoing professional development for principals to sharpen their leadership competencies and increase their efficacy. Like doctors, school leaders require a dedication to lifelong learning. A doctor's education and training begin in elementary school and continues throughout the physician's career. Physicians continue to learn by participating in continuing education activities. After medical school, physicians undertake up to seven years of graduate medical education. Medical professionals protect our health and save our lives. Principals and school leaders are responsible for the educational lives of our children. I consider the responsibility for saving the futures of our children on par with that of the medical profession.

We must focus the same attention to improving the instructional decision-making and practice of principals that the medical profession provides for their doctors.

My hope is that this book, written from the mind and heart of one who has paid her dues as a principal, will challenge the policymakers at the state, agency, district, and board levels to: 1) restructure the school system so that the professional development programs support the ongoing leadership needs of principals; 2) adopt leadership coaching as the strategy that is implemented on-site, based on self-determined needs by the principals; 3) provide leadership coaching as ongoing follow-up support designed to enable our principals to transfer these effective leadership skills in a way which impacts teachers and students in our nation's classrooms.

Lovelady School Leadership Consulting was formed to provide this service to principals and leadership teams. Our mission is to offer on-site coaching to principals that is site-specific and ongoing in the areas of Assessment, Curriculum, and Instruction. We believe that these three areas have direct impact on teaching and learning.

We all can agree that whatever else occurs in education, at any level, the primary determinant for student success is an effective teacher. But despite the focus on staff development training of teachers and principals, school systems are still failing to meet their responsibilities to students. From my experience, it is my firm belief that we will not see transformation on a significant level until staff development practices include a systematic approach for the onsite, site-specific and ongoing leadership coaching of the school principal. When principals are well prepared and properly supported to lead their schools, the impact on teacher effectiveness and student achievement is positive and significant.

Conclusion

To successfully improve schools, principals need to be empowered to develop new characteristics and behaviors required to lead their schools through effective change and improvement. A commitment of support from all levels will communicate a message to principals that their leadership needs are a priority. I believe that the need is so great that we have no other option than to change the leadership professional paradigm so that **no principal is left behind**.

Please Note:

Chapter 8 is designed to be used as a workbook. You will find tools, techniques and other resources to be used as you systematically implement the 5 Phases of the School Principal Change Model™. Each exercise will provide an in-depth understanding of the major components in the Model.

Make use of these resources as you work with your staff and parents. All presentation outlines and activities are reproducible. Please visit MyCoach Interactive™ at www.LoveladySchoolLeadership.com to download presentations and activities.

CHAPTER 8

Tools, Techniques and Other Resources

"Practice does not make perfect. Only perfect practice makes perfect."
—Vince Lombardi

The Play Book: "You Can Do It!"

In this section, you will find valuable presentations and activities to support you as you begin your journey to change and transformation. The tools, techniques and resources complement each phase of the School Principal Change Model™. Other resources are provided to highlight key concepts. Both sections are designed to coach you on your understanding of the change process outlined in the book.

Reproducibles of all activities and presentations in this section may be downloaded from MyCoach Interactive™ at www.LoveladySchoolLeadership.com.

Sections contain:

1. A presentation outline – Introduces the main concept of each phase of the School Principal Change Model™. You can download the actual presentation on MyCoach Interactive™ to use with your teams.

2. Activity – The activities follow a presentation and are designed to coach you through facilitating change in your school with your leadership team.

PRESENTATION AND GROUP ACTIVITY FACILITATION TIPS

Contact participants in advance and assure that they understand the purpose of the meeting and their role. If they are disinterested or if they appear to have an "agenda" that might affect group productivity, now is the best time to deal with it.

Publish an agenda well in advance. Set reasonable expectations for the first meeting. For instance, unless the problem is narrow in scope and already well understood, you may wish to limit the first meeting's agenda to writing a mission statement and creating a data-gathering plan.

Select a meeting place that is comfortable, well ventilated, quiet, away from distractions, and offers plenty of space to hang flip chart pages on the walls. For meetings longer than an hour or two, consider providing beverages and snacks.

Stock the meeting room with several flip charts, plenty of fresh markers, and "tent cards" on which participants can write their names.

Start promptly, and generally respect people's time. Allow for breaks but adjust the timing according to group progress: It is okay to delay a break – briefly – if the group is nearing closure on a difficult task. Make it clear that you will start promptly again after a break.

Allow time for introductions. Besides name and role, asking participants to provide a thought or two related to the purpose or their expectations of the meeting helps set a businesslike tone and may surface misunderstandings or hidden agendas early. Beware of "ice breaker" activities that are unrelated to the business of the meeting, since these tend to distract attention and may cause busy participants to feel that their time is being wasted.

How to Create a Shared Vision — Phase 1

This exercise contains three activities with three associated visuals for your entire school improvement team. If you have staff development days, we recommend you allocate a full day (approximately 8 hours) of interrupted time to complete the entire process (presenting the PowerPoint, completing activities and group work). If you do not have full days as an option, you may use several staff development meetings to complete this activity.

HOW TO DO THIS ACTIVITY

This "visioneering" exercise requires individual work, smaller group work and larger group participation.

The larger group will select a "wordsmith" team and a "creative" team. At the start of the meeting, ask for approximately 5 volunteers who enjoy writing and others who enjoy graphic design, art and are creative. The "wordsmith" team will take the adopted draft vision statement and finalize it for adoption by the entire school. After the vision has been adopted, the "creative" team will determine how to publicize the new school vision, both in the school and in the community.

In forming smaller work groups, use a system to create random groups such as counting off participants 1-5. Instruct each small group to sit together and ask them to select a recorder and a small group facilitator.

Establish ground rules for participants. You may start with these, but allow participants to add to list:

- Speak one at a time
- Listen to understand, not to argue
- Respect one another
- Observe time limits
- Everyone participates; no one dominates

How to Develop a Shared Vision Presentation

What is a Vision?

A vision statement is a description of a school's aspirations. It describes what the school would like to achieve in the future.

The vision statement is intended to serve as a clear roadmap for current and future actions.

What is the difference between Vision and Mission?

- Vision – Visioning activities are about the "aspirational dreams"
- Mission – Missioning activities are about translating the vision into SMART goalposts

What are SMART goals?

- Strategic/Specific
- Measurable
- Attainable
- Results-Oriented
- Time-bound

    (O'Neill & Corzemius, 2006)

What is the value of a Shared Vision?

- Developing a shared vision statement is one way for a team to determine the direction in which they will go
- The vision can serve as inspiration and hope; it can engender commitment and loyalty
- It can serve as the foundation for goal-setting and action-planning

What are the steps to develop a Shared Vision?

- Determine who will participate. Schedule a staff meeting to include the entire school community in the implementation of the vision.

- Make adequate preparation. Schedule at least (1) full day or several segments of several days to equal approximately 8 hours. Consider a day when students are not in attendance in order to avoid interruptions. Also consider using a neutral "facilitator." That will remove the principal from being the focal point and will help ideas flow freely.

- Determine appropriate "input" to the vision. Schedule the meeting far enough ahead of time to allow for adequate preparation, research, data analysis and other information-gathering needed to prepare participants. Send out documents and require that participants read them.

- Set the stage. Review the desired outcomes, agenda, process and ground rules. Check for understanding and agreement. Doing this models collaboration and consensus.

How do I involve my team in developing a Shared Vision?

- Group Activity
- Divide into groups of 3-4, select a facilitator and someone to take notes
- Brainstorm answers to questions, record ideas, draw pictures, create phrases and anything else to describe that desired future. Allocate 30 minutes.
- Groups report to the larger group
- Lead facilitator records key phrases on flip chart, periodically asking clarifying questions
- Rank by tallying the votes for each phrase
- Prioritize in the same manner
- Group Activity follow-up
- Appoint a sub-committee to write the draft vision statement
- Send the draft to the entire team for feedback
- Incorporate feedback and publish the vision statement

How do I make sure everyone knows about our new Shared Vision?

- Publicize your new Vision
- Display the vision statement in numerous creative ways

What ideas do you have to publicize your new vision?

SAMPLE –
How to Create a Shared Vision Meeting Agenda

8:00 – 8:30   Refreshments

8:30 – 9:30   Introductions
- Establish the objective for the day
- Predict outcomes for the day
- Review Agenda (Make sure the schedule for the day is clearly posted.) Explain the rules and the protocol
- Use a system to establish mini-groups (count 1-5, all 1's in same group, etc. Assign a facilitator for each group
- Distribute the activity sheets and explain how they are to be used
- Facilitator explains Visual #1
- Entire team completes Activity #1 (this will not be shared), Facilitator summarizes Visual #2
- Smaller groups will break out into separate workgroups

9:30 – 10:30   Smaller groups will revisit all visuals
- Complete Activity #2

10:30 – 12:00 Capture summary of Activity #2 on poster paper to report to the larger-group
- Post work in the larger meeting area

12:00 – 1:00   Break for lunch (consider a potluck to get your team involved)

1:00 – 2:00   Each group shares Activity #2 summary with the larger group
- Main facilitator shares Visual #3 and instructs group to break again into small groups to work on the creation of their version of a vision statement

2:00 – 3:00   Break into smaller groups to complete Activity #3
- Summarize group vision statement on poster paper to report to the larger group

3:00 – 3:30   Each group presents their Vision Statement
- Larger group decides on one or combines several parts

3:30   Give draft statement to the "wordsmith" team to finalize. (Once the statement is final, the "word smith" team will give the document to the "creative" team)

How to Create a Shared Vision Activity

Visual #1:

Present this visual to stimulate conversation among group participants. Set the stage for Activity #1 where individuals will identify their core beliefs.

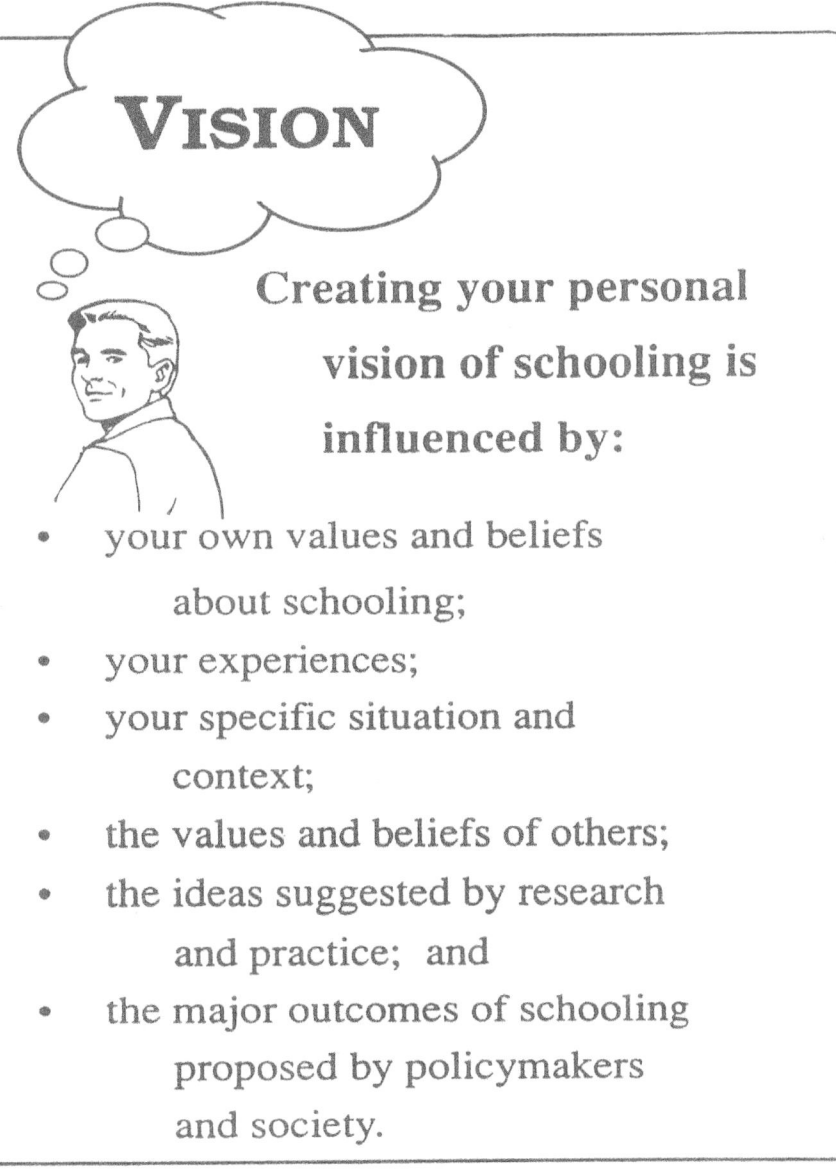

Ask participants the following questions for discussion:

What insight would you like to share regarding identifiable values and beliefs about schooling?

_____
_____
_____
_____
_____
_____
_____
_____
_____
_____

What are your experiences and your specific insights regarding how a leader might act upon his/her beliefs?

_____
_____
_____
_____
_____
_____
_____
_____
_____
_____
_____

Activity #1:
Identifying Individual Core Beliefs

This activity is designed to help individuals understand what visualization requires, by identifying their own belief systems. The activity requires you to establish what you believe in. The questions guide you through a process that is connected to the school.

Please complete the following exercise:

I believe that...

1. Schools should teach

_____
_____
_____
_____
_____
_____
_____
_____

2. A good school is one that

_____
_____
_____
_____
_____
_____
_____
_____

3. A successful student is able to

_____
_____
_____
_____
_____
_____
_____
_____

4. An effective classroom is one in which

_____
_____
_____
_____
_____
_____
_____
_____

5. A good school/central office staff member (i.e., teacher, principal, supervisor) is one who

_____
_____
_____
_____
_____
_____
_____
_____

6. An effective school/faculty/central office is one that

_____
_____
_____
_____
_____
_____
_____
_____

7. A quality instructional program includes

_____
_____
_____
_____
_____
_____
_____
_____

Visual #2 – Insights

Visual #2 is presented to participants after Activity #1 is completed. Discuss this visual and capture thoughts.

Leaders <u>can</u> make difference in student learning because…

They have strong identifiable values and beliefs about schooling

<u>and</u>

They are capable and willing to act upon their values and beliefs.

Ask participants the following questions for discussion:

1. What insight would you like to share after reading this?

   _____
   _____
   _____
   _____
   _____
   _____
   _____
   _____
   _____
   _____
   _____
   _____

2. What are your experiences and your specific insights?

   _____
   _____
   _____
   _____
   _____
   _____
   _____
   _____
   _____

Activity #2:
Small Group Activity

Please complete the following exercise.

Describe your ideal school. If you were watching the activities in your ideal school:

1. What would you see?

   _____
   _____
   _____
   _____
   _____
   _____
   _____
   _____
   _____
   _____
   _____

2. What would you see students doing?

   _____
   _____
   _____
   _____
   _____
   _____
   _____
   _____
   _____

3. What would you see teachers doing?

_____
_____
_____
_____
_____
_____
_____
_____

4. What would you see administrators doing?

_____
_____
_____
_____
_____
_____
_____
_____

5. What would you see parents or community members doing?

_____
_____
_____
_____
_____
_____
_____
_____

Visual #3:
Sample Vision Statement

Below is a sample vision statement. Present to group. Ask participants to share any brief thoughts about this sample vision statement. Following the discussion, break into smaller groups for Activity #3.

> *"Let us put our minds together and see what life we will make for our children."*
>
> *— Sitting Bull, Lakota*

Write down your thoughts about this example vision statement.

_____
_____
_____
_____
_____
_____
_____
_____
_____
_____
_____

Activity #3:
Developing the Vision Statement

The first part of this exercise is designed to be completed in smaller groups. The objective is to create a Vision Statement for your school. Use Visual #3 as an idea starter.

Steps:

1. Brainstorm and write down ideas on chart paper
2. Rank and prioritize all ideas
3. From the prioritized list, create a vision statement on flipchart paper to share with the larger group

The second part of this exercise should be completed in the larger group.

Steps:

1. Facilitator requests that each group post and share their vision statement
2. The entire group then selects one or takes good ideas from each to make one vision statement
3. The "wordsmith" team is assigned the vision statement to clean it up and put it in draft form
4. At the next school improvement team meeting, the "wordsmith" team reports and asks for consensus
5. Vision statement is adopted
6. The vision statement is assigned to the "creative" team to determine how they are going to post and communicate the new school vision (i.e., in libraries, stores, website, bags in the grocery store, billboards, painted on school walls, charts for classrooms, newsletter, letterhead, handbook, handouts for parents, etc.)

Congratulations! Your new school vision reflects the core values of your entire school improvement team.

Now Celebrate!

How to Develop a School Mission Statement Presentation – Phase 2

When is the Mission Statement developed?

- The mission statement is developed after forming the vision statement and describes *what* the group is going to do and *why*.

What is a School Mission Statement?

- Provides overall direction
- Clarifies your purpose and meaning
- Enables you to know clearly what you want to be and do in your life

Allows you to feel:

— strong in your sense of mission

— in control

— powerful

— deeply committed

— committed to your innermost values

Why is a School Mission Statement important?

- Provides overall direction and clarifies the school's Purpose and Meaning
- Represents the school's belief system, priorities, values, principles
- Helps you decide if what you offer, and the way you provide it lines up with your educational goals

What does Stephen R. Covey, author of <u>The 7 Habits of Highly Effective People</u> and <u>First Things First</u> say about developing a Mission Statement?

- Sees the construct of our mission statement as a way to cultivate "the passion of vision."

- Describes such a mission statement as "a motivating force so powerful, it, in effect, becomes the DNA of our lives."
- Declares it is so engrained and integrated into every aspect of our being that it becomes the compelling impetus behind every decision we make.
- Determines that this passion can empower us literally to transcend fear, doubt, discouragement and many other things that keep up from accomplishment and contribution.

What does creating a mission statement require?

- Thoughtful introspection
- Careful analysis
- Deep soul-searching

What questions should be asked before creating a school mission statement?

- Are we committed to providing high-quality education?
- Are we fair, honest, courteous, and professional in our relationships with:
    — Our students?
    — Our fellow teachers?
    — Our administrators?
    — Our staff?
    — Our parents?
    — Our community?
- Are we sensitive to our students' needs and dedicated to their success?
- Do we provide our students opportunities to grow and feel motivated in their accomplishments?
- Are we a symbol of leadership and active participation in our community?

Sample Mission Statements

1. **Shonto Preparatory School** PO Box 70, Shonto AZ 86054

   "It is our mission to become and remain the finest School District in the State of Arizona and on the Navajo Nation by ensuring that each student becomes all that he or she is capable of being while respecting cultural and traditional values."

   School Description

   Based in Shonto, Arizona on the Navajo Nation Reservation, Shonto Preparatory School offers preschool to middle school students a full academic and sports program for Navajo students and other students that attend our school.

2. **Community School** 7815 Williamson Rd., Roanoke, VA 24019

   "Community School recognizes that each child is an individual; that all children are creative; that all children need to succeed; therefore, Community School respects the individual needs of children; fosters a caring and creative environment; and emphasizes the social, emotional, physical, intellectual development of each child."

   Description

   Based in Roanoke, Virginia, the Community School offers education from preschool to middle school for all children of different racial, cultural, religious, and economic backgrounds.

3. **Princeton Academy of the Sacred Heart** 1128 Great Rd., Princeton, NJ 08540

   "Our mission is to develop young men with active and creative minds, a sense of understanding and compassion for others, and the courage to act on their beliefs. We stress the total development of each child: spiritual, moral, intellectual, social, emotional, and physical."

   Description

   The Princeton Academy of the Sacred Heart is an exclusive Catholic school for boys who are in lower and middle school. They not only focus on academics but also on the context of faith.

How to Create a School Mission Statement and School Motto

This is an activity for your entire school improvement team, parents and other community members.

We recommended that you conduct these exercises over 2 faculty meetings. There are two objectives:

1. To create the mission statement
2. To create the school motto

How to do this activity

In the first meeting, present the "How to create a school mission statement" presentation and complete activity questions provided. Like the vision statement activity, the mission statement activities should be completed in small and large groups. Segment work groups by grade levels for elementary and middle school, and by content area for high schools. Groups will brainstorm ideas for the mission statement. Each group presents their mission statement in the larger group. Specifically you should:

1. Segment into 5 smaller groups
   - Establish group facilitators and notetakers
2. Individuals in each group complete the Activity #1 questions
3. Each group discusses who they are as a school and a community
4. Use the samples of how to create a mission statement from the presentation
5. Each group then brainstorms a mission statement and documents it
6. Return to general session and report each group's mission statement
7. Decide and vote on the one that best describes the purpose of the school

The goal of the second meeting and activity is to create 5 banners representing a motto that expresses the adopted mission statement. The same small 5 work groups that created the mission statement will work together again to create a hanging felt banner that expresses the school motto.

Each workgroup presents their banner to the larger group. All banners will be placed around the school.

Definitions

What is a motto?

- The motto is a cheer, a saying or a rallying cry that will engender a positive spirit within the school team and infuse energy into the school. The motto helps to create a culture of cooperation and collaboration in the school. It focuses the school on the mission. It creates a friendly climate that motivates the school (principal, teachers, staff, students, parents and community) to work together as a team.

How is the motto used?

- The motto is displayed all over the school in classrooms, halls, at sports events, at assemblies and in local businesses. It is designed to create a climate of teamwork within the school community at large.

- These activities are designed to create a learning community. These activities enable participants to work as a group to impact and change, if necessary, the school culture; to take ownership and become accountable for the success of the school.

Day 1 Activity #1 –
How to Create a School Mission Statement

Each person individually completes the following questions. Participants will then share their answers. The recorder will write all unduplicated answers on chart paper as each person contributes. The facilitator and recorder will be prepared to present at larger group assembly.

1. What is a mission statement?

   _____
   _____
   _____
   _____
   _____

2. Why should you create a mission statement?

   _____
   _____
   _____
   _____
   _____

3. Create a mission statement and be prepared to share with your group.

   _____
   _____
   _____
   _____
   _____

Day 2 Activity #2
—How to Create a School Motto

Break into the same small groups used for Mission Statement Development Statement and follow steps 6-9 below:

Step 1 Brainstorm questions and document answers.

Step 2 Rank and prioritize ideas.

Step 3 Develop a Mission Statement and obtain consensus.

Step 4 Be prepared to share your Mission Statement with all staff.

Step 5 Determine by consensus which Mission Statement will be adopted (Combine, Omit, Clarify)

Group Work (Same Groupings)

Step 6 Use the materials provided and create a Mission Banner that best represents the spirit of your newly adopted Mission Statement.

Step 7 Be prepared to present your group's Mission Banner to all staff.

Step 8 Determine which Mission Banner best expresses your values and goals most clearly and why.

Step 9 Determine where your Mission Banner will be placed.

Materials* needed for motto construction:

- 5 long felt banners in 5 different colors. Cut 1 for each team.
- 15 4x10 squares of felt in various colors. Distribute 3 per team.

Cotton balls	5 dowels
Ice cream sticks	Strong string to hang banner
Glitter	Toothpicks
Glue	4x4 cards
Multi-colored pencils	Paint
Aluminum foil	Beads
Post-it-notes	Paperclips
Felt pens in various color	

Add any assortment of materials from the inside and outside environment that you desire for this exercise.

How to Plan for Action Presentation – Phase 3

Why should I plan for action?

Action Planning is an analytical process that brings structure and prevents you from wasting time doing the wrong thing.

Concrete strategy for action planning allows leadership teams to focus on their purpose and goals, as well as produce written plans and documentation that can be used to persuade others, garner resources, and move forward.

What do I do first?

Create an Action Plan

What is an Action Plan?

The Action Plan is the written documentation of the prescription or remedy determined by the work of the school improvement team.

What is the Purpose of an Action Plan?

The purpose of an Action Plan is to organize and develop strategic solutions to address a specific issue, challenge or problem.

Why should a school principal or leadership team conduct strategic planning?

- To engage the entire community in preparing for change
- To capture the goals of the school community in an orderly and efficient manner
- To encourage the school community to share in the achievement of the goals
- To promote the efficient use of the school and community organizational resources

What are the steps to creating an Action Plan?

1. Define your mission

- The mission statement answers three questions:
    1. What are you going to do?

2. For whom?

3. To what end?

2. *Gather data on the problem and describe it*
   - This step establishes and implements a plan for gathering background data
   - Gather data on the problem and describe the problem you want to solve – Where are you starting?
   - Recognize that at the start of the planning cycle, your picture of the problem is incomplete

3. *Determine the critical success factors (CSFs)*
   - This step establishes and implements a plan for gathering background data.
   - The purpose of this step is to consider what must go right in order for your project to succeed and, conversely, what factors will ensure failure should they not be addressed. Gather data on the problem and describe the problem you want to solve – Where are you starting?

4. *Establish your goals – make them SMART*
   - **S**pecific, **M**easurable, **A**ttainable, **R**esults-oriented, **T**ime-bound
   - Ask, "What are my goals?"
   - Objectives need to be focused, measurable, and constrained by time limits.
   - The key to an objective is that the results are tangible and unambiguously observable.

5. *Set Objectives, Target Dates, and Measures*
   - Ask, "What are the tasks needed to achieve my objectives?"
     1. The outcome of this step is a final plan document

2. Remember, your plan still requires careful analysis and description of the actions to be taken, by whom, and when

3. Defining action steps is a vital final step

What are the 5 elements of each step?

1. Step Name and Overview

    - A description of what is to be accomplished in that step

2. Directions

    - Detailed directions to accomplish the step including sub-steps

3. Deliverables

    - The work products of each step

4. Measures

    - The means by which the quality of each step can be assured

5. Facilitation Tips

    - Hints for successfully working the step in a group setting

How to Plan for Activity Sheet Excercises A-H (1,2 and 3)

An activity for your entire school improvement team.

This activity includes a series of worksheets (Appendices A through H) for you to capture your work as you proceed through the steps of creating your action plan.

Some information you will enter on the worksheets is relevant only to that step. Think of these entries as intermediate work products. Other entries, such as your mission statement, you will carry forward to the final worksheet, which is the Action Plan.

The Action Plan (Appendix H, pages 1-3) is a summary of the preceding worksheets A - G. The Action Plan is organized to enable your school improvement team to rapidly grasp your intent. The summary communicates what is expected of them and what they can expect of you and others. It also communicates when goals will be achieved and how they, as a school improvement team, contribute to achieving the overall mission.

Action Planning: Mission

Project: _____

This is a step to solve a problem you have identified and is a separate activity from creating a school mission statement.

1. Brainstorm the answers to these three questions:

(Products or Services) What are you going to do?	*(Customers)* For whom?	*(Purpose)* To what end?

2. Use your brainstormed lists to draft a mission statement that answers all three questions.

Mission Worksheet - Appendix A

Lovelady School Leadership Consulting ©2011 Reproducible

Action Planning: Data-gathering Plan   Project: _____

1. In the columns below, create your plan to capture the data you need to understand the current state.

(Data Requirements and Priority) What questions do you need to answer? How important is the answer to each? 1. Essential 2. Valuable 3. Useful Background	*(People, Documents, etc.)* Where can you find the answers?	*(Responsibility and Deadlines)* Who will gather the information? When?

Data-gathering Plan Worksheet - Appendix B

Lovelady School Leadership Consulting ©2011 Reproducible

Action Planning: Current State Report   Project: _____

1. Record the details of your data-gathering in the blocks below.

(Data-gathering Questions) What did you ask?	*(Data)* What did you learn?

2. Summarize what you learned in a few brief statements.

Current State Report Worksheet - Appendix C

Lovelady School Leadership Consulting ©2011 Reproducible

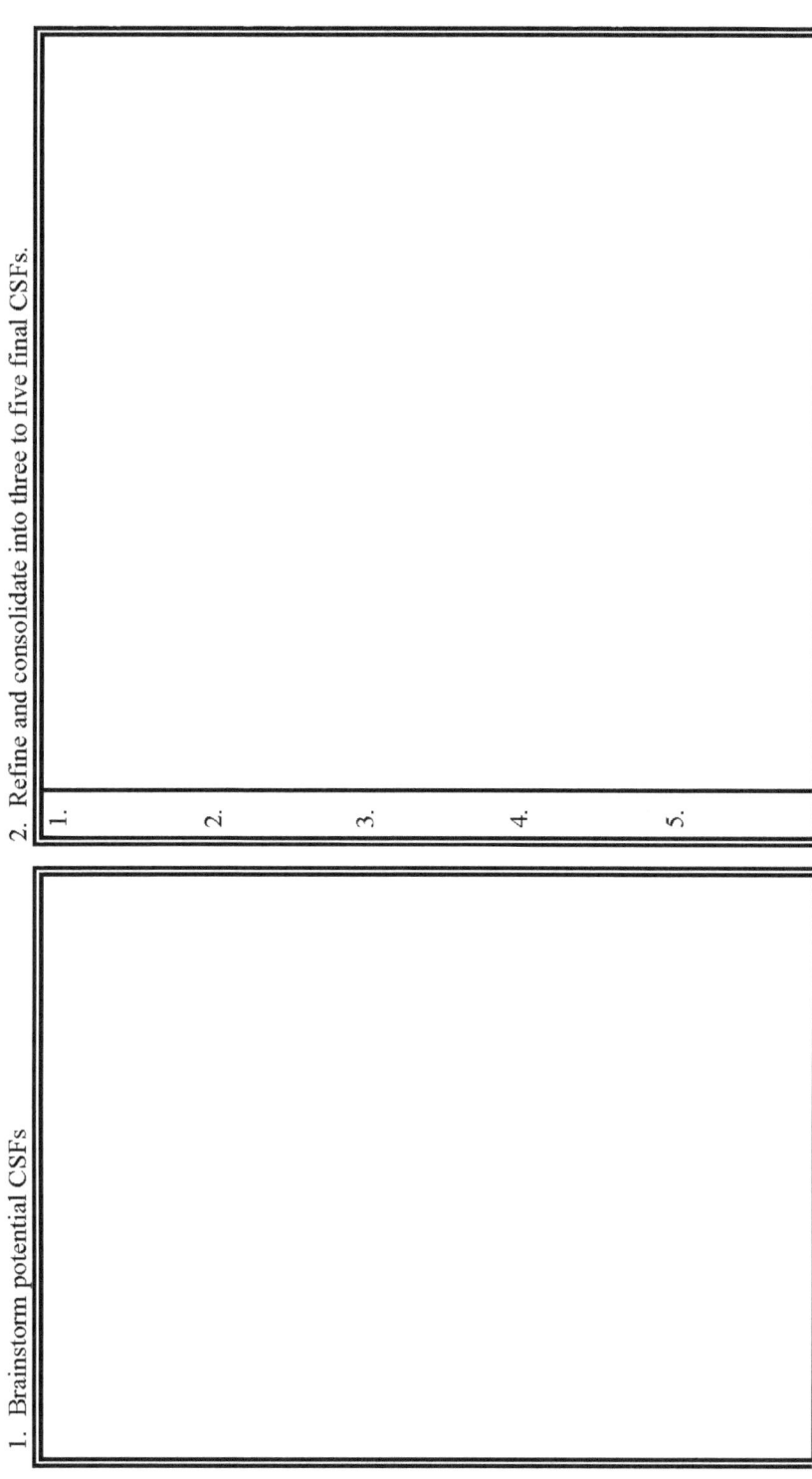

Action Planning: Fundamental Components   Project: _____

Reminder: Identify fundamental components asking, "which means?" or "which requires?" of each Critical Success Factor (CSF).

1. Use one sheet for each CSF.
2. Enter the CSF Number on the line and text of the CSF in the block
3. Use the space below the block to draw in smaller blocks for the fundamental components, attaching them by lines to each other. (Your finished diagram should look something like an organizational chart.)

CSF Number: ___

Fundamental Components Worksheet - Appendix E

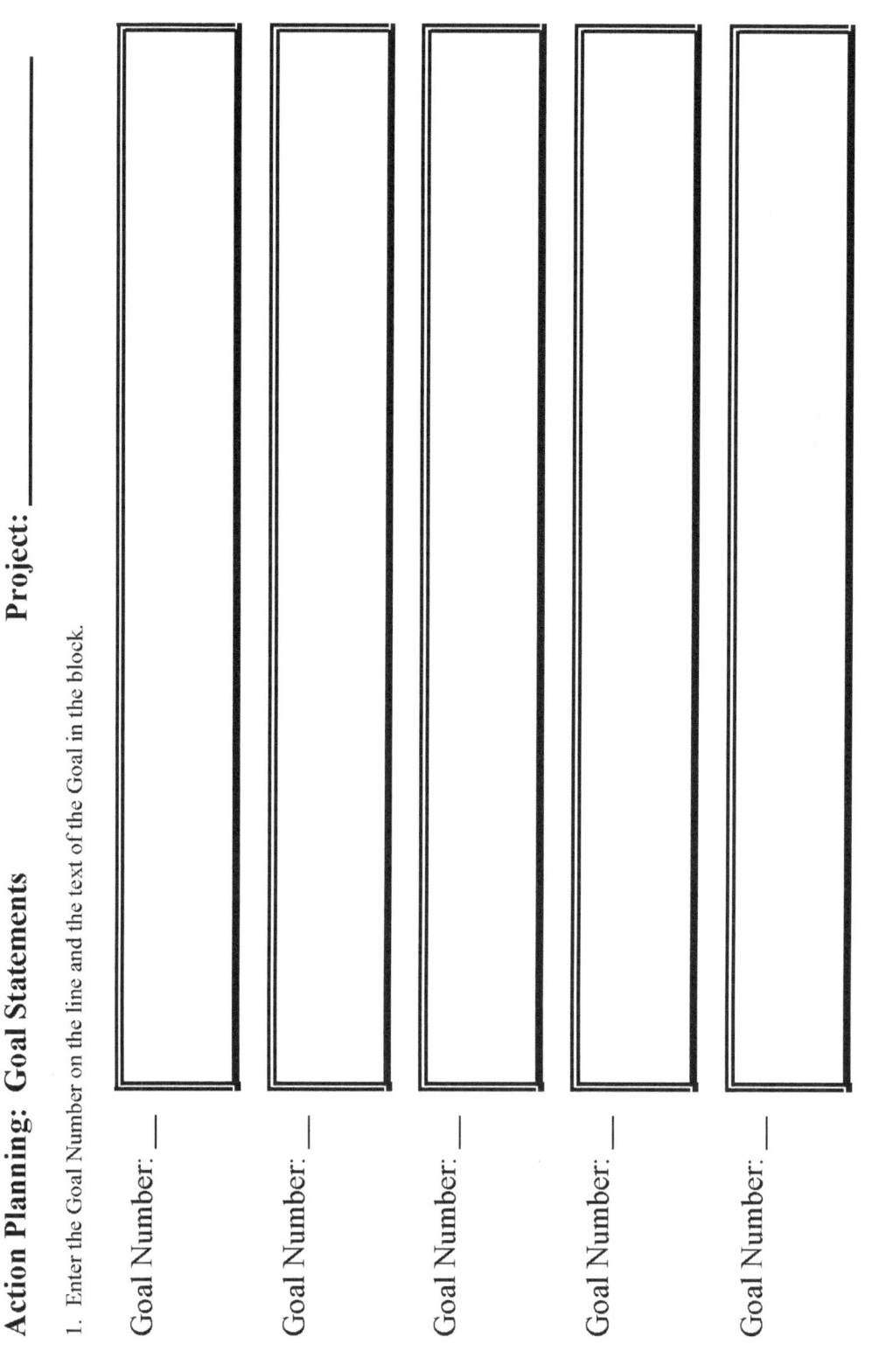

Action Planning: Objectives and Measures   Project: _____

1. Enter the Goal Number in the space and text of the Goal in the block.

Goal Number: ___

2. Enter objectives to achieve each goal. Include target dates and measures of success for each.

(Objectives) What must you accomplish?	*(Target Dates)* By when?	*(Measures)* How will you measure success?

Objectives and Measures Worksheet - Appendix G

Lovelady School Leadership Consulting ©2011 Reproducible

Action Planning Worksheet

Project: _____

Prepared by: _____

Date: _____

Mission:

Current State Summary:

Critical Success Factors (CSFs)

Action Planning Worksheet – Appendix H, page 1 of 3

Lovelady School Leadership Consulting ©2011 Reproducible

Goal No.: __

Objectives for this Goal:

(Objectives) What outcome do you wish to achieve?	*(Target Dates)* By when?	*(Measures)* How will you measure success?

Action Planning Worksheet - Appendix H, page 2 of 3

Lovelady School Leadership Consulting ©2011 Reproducible

Objective No.: ___

Action Steps to achieve this objective:

What must be done? (Action)	By whom? (Responsibility)	Starting? (Start Date)	Completed? (Due Date)	Comments: (Contingencies, resources, etc.)

Action Planning Worksheet - Appendix H, page 3 of 3

Lovelady School Leadership Consulting ©2011 Reproducible

How to Take Action Presentation — Phase 4

What do I need to know about how to Take Action?
Taking Action Requires the Team to Work as a Group

How should I organize this activity?

The principal's role is to orchestrate the steps the team will take by issuing written instructions as follows:

- Schedule a series of meetings for action tasks and disseminate dates to your entire team
- Administer the How to Take Action Teamwork Survey provided
- Score and determine your team's stage of teamwork
- Discuss and make plans to improve or maintain teamwork as reflected in your score

What should I do during the process?
- Refer to the written plan and determine what objectives will be addressed
- Determine what research needs to be done for specific objectives
- Determine what additional staff skills are needed
- Schedule staff trainings as needed

What should the team understand about the Action Plan?
- What the Action Plan contains
- Why an Action Plan is needed
- How the Action Plan works
- Who is responsible for taking action
- When specific actions are to be taken

How do I ensure this process is successful?

- In your meetings, use the Triple T process to document decisions. It is simple, but sufficient to provide the information needed in this step:

    Task—What is the objective?

    Talent—Who is responsible?

    Timeline—When will it begin? When will it end?

- Schedule monitoring meetings to receive and give feedback regarding how well the implementation of the Action Plan is progressing
- Consider contracting the services of an Expert School Leadership Coach
- Assign the Leadership Coach as an additional expert monitor for the implementation of the Action Plan
- The Leadership Coach can also participate in the Observation/Feedback process for this step to ensure support instructional success

How to Take Action Activity

Before you begin working as a group to take action, complete the teamwork survey. Use the key to evaluate your team's stage of development. Make a plan to address areas of need.

Objectives

To identify the present stage of the teamwork at which your team is operating.

Directions

This questionnaire contains statements about teamwork. Next to each question mark how often your team displays each behavior by using the following scoring system:

- Almost never - 1
- Seldom - 2
- Occasionally - 3
- Frequently - 4
- Almost always - 5

Questionnaire

_____ 1. We have set procedures or protocols to ensure that things are orderly and run smoothly (e.g., minimize interruptions; everyone gets the opportunity to have their say).

_____ 2. We are quick to get on with the task on hand and do not spend too much time in the planning stage.

_____ 3. Our team believes that we are all in it together and shares responsibilities for the team's success or failure.

_____ 4. We have thorough procedures for agreeing on our objectives and planning the way we will perform our tasks.

_____ 5. Team members are afraid or do not like to ask others for help.

_____ 6. We take our team's goals and objectives literally, and assume a shared understanding.

_____ 7. The team leader keeps order and contributes to the task at hand.

_____ 8. We do not have fixed procedures; we make them up as the task or project progresses.

_____ 9. We generate lots of ideas, but we do not use many because we fail to listen to them and reject them without fully understanding them.

_____ 10. Team members do not fully trust the other members and closely monitor others who are working on a specific task.

_____ 11. The team leader ensures that we follow the procedures, do not argue, do not interrupt, and keep to the point.

_____ 12. We enjoy working together; we have a fun and productive time.

_____ 13. We have accepted each other as members of the team.

_____ 14. The team leader is democratic and collaborative.

_____ 15. We are working to define the goal and what tasks need to be accomplished.

_____ 16. Many of the team members have their own ideas about the process, and personal agendas are rampant.

_____ 17. We fully accept each other's strengths and weaknesses.

_____ 18. We assign specific roles to team members (team leader, facilitator, timekeeper, note-taker, etc.).

_____ 19. We achieve harmony by avoiding conflict.

_____ 20. The tasks are quite different from what we imagined and seem difficult to accomplish.

_____ 21. Many abstract discussions of the concepts and issues take place, which makes some members impatient with these discussions.

_____ 22. We are able to work through group problems.

_____ 23. We argue a lot, even though we agree on the real issues.

_____ 24. The team is often tempted to go above the original scope of the project.

_____ 25. We express criticism of others constructively.

_____ 26. There is a close attachment to the team.

_____ 27. Little is being accomplished with the project's goals.

_____ 28. The goals we have established seem unrealistic.

_____ 29. Although we are not fully sure of the project's goals and issues, we are excited and proud to be on the team.

_____ 30. We often share personal problems with each other.

_____ 31. Team members resist the tasks at hand and any quality-improvement approaches.

_____ 32. We get a lot of work done.

Part 2 - Scoring

Next to each survey item number below, transfer the score that you gave that item on the questionnaire. For example, if you scored item one with a 3 (Occasionally), enter a 3 next to item 1 below. When you have entered all the scores for each question, total each of the four columns.

Item	Score	Item	Score	Item	Score	Item	Score
1.		2.		4.		3.	
5.		7.		6.		8.	
10.		9.		11.		12.	
15.		16.		13.		14.	
18.		20.		19.		17.	
21.		23.		24.		22.	
27.		28.		25.		26.	
29.		31.		30.		32.	
TOTAL		**TOTAL**		**TOTAL**		**TOTAL**	
Forming Stage		Storming Stage		Norming Stage		Performing Stage	

This questionnaire is to help you assess what stage your team normally operates from. It is based on the "Tuckman" model of Forming, Storming, Norming, and Performing. The lowest score possible for a stage is 8 (Almost never) while the highest score possible for a stage is 40 (Almost always).

The highest of the four scores indicates which stage you perceive your team to normally operate from. If your highest score is 32 or more, it is a strong indicator of the stage your team is in.

The lowest of the three scores is an indicator of the stage your team is least like. If your lowest score is 16 or less, it is a strong indicator that your team does not operate this way.

If two of the scores are close to the same, you are probably going through a transition phase, except:

- If you score high in both the Forming and Storming Phases, then you are in the Storming Phase
- If you score high in both the Norming and Performing Phases, then you are in the Performing Stage

A small difference between three or four scores indicates that you have no clear perception of the way your team operates, the team's performance is highly variable, or that you are in the Storming phase (this phase can be extremely volatile, with high and low points).

Source: Clark, D. (2004).

Key - Teamwork survey

The progression is:

1. Forming
2. Storming
3. Norming
4. Performing

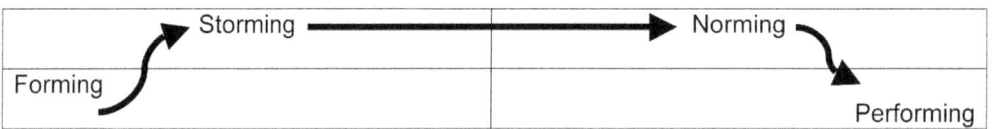

Forming – Stage 1

High dependence on leader for guidance and direction. Little agreement on team aims. Individual roles and responsibilities are unclear. Process is often ignored. Leader directs in "telling mode."

Storming – Stage 2

Decisions do not come easily within group. Team members vie for position. Clarity of purpose increases, but uncertainties persist. Cliques and factions form, and there may be power struggles. The team needs to focus on goals to avoid distractions and emotional issues. Compromises may be required to enable progress. Leader coaches in "selling mode."

Norming – Stage 3

Agreement and consensus forms among team, who responds to facilitation by leader. Roles and responsibilities are clear and accepted. Big decisions are made by group agreement. Smaller decisions may be delegated to individuals or smaller groups within team. Commitment and unity are strong. The team may engage in fun and social activities. The team discusses and develops its processes and working style. There is general respect for the leader and some of the leadership is shared by the team. Leader facilitates and enables in "participating mode."

Performing – Stage 4

The team is more strategically aware. The team knows clearly why it is doing what it is doing. The team has a shared vision and is able to stand on its own feet with no interference or participation from the leader. There is a focus on over-achieving goals. The team makes most decisions based on criteria agreed upon with the leader. The team has a high degree of autonomy. Disagreements occur but they are resolved positively within the team. The team is able to work toward achieving the goal. Team members look after each other. The team requires delegated tasks from leader but does not need to be instructed or assisted. Team members may ask for assistance for personal and professional development. Leader delegates and oversees in "delegating mode."

How to Take Action Implementation Plan

Use this form to create your action implementation plan. Use Action Step Worksheet Appendix H from Action Planning Exercises to guide this completion.

Give a concise name for this plan or objective from Appendix H.

_____
_____

Briefly state the desired results to be achieved and strategies to be used.

_____
_____
_____
_____
_____
_____
_____
_____

What are the key strengths, weaknesses, opportunities and threats to this plan?

Strengths	Weaknesses
Opportunities	Threats

Who are the people that will work together on this effort?

Name	Skill/Resources	Email	Phone

What are some of the important tasks to be completed to make this a success? Focus on the immediate <u>start-up work required and major milestones</u> to be reached.

Task	Who is responsible?	By When?	Cost/Resources

How to Get Results Presentation – Phase 5

How do I get results?

To get results, the principal and the leadership team must take the lead in setting up the environment for learning.

What are the benefits of this process?

— Eliminates the barriers to learning

— Sets up individual and organizational learning strategies

— Gets strategically aligned

— Makes a plan

What are the barriers to getting results?

Inertia

- Protection of the status quo, "I can't be changed…"

Bureaucracy

- Rules, regulations, red tape that keeps you from progressing

Self-Preservation

- "…but I've taught this same class for 30 years the same way."

Organizational Structure

- "Our guidelines cannot accommodate your idea."

Established Culture

- "That's not the way we do things around here."

Miscellaneous

- "We'll find some reason why we don't like it."

How should I set this process up?

Set up individual and organizational learning strategies

Individual

— Reflecting on experience

— Coaching

— Learning teams

— Mentoring

— Special Assignments

— Self-development

— Individual development plan (IDP)

Organizational

— Action learning

— Cross-functional teams

— Work-outs (Staff at all levels in a Professional Learning Community (PLC) to seek answers to a problem)

— Strategic planning

— Study group

— Bench-marking

— "Flocking" – patterns of self-organization

— Groupware (technology support)

— Computer conferencing

How do I get the team strategically aligned?

Align trainings and learning activities with your mission and goals by:

— Reviewing your school's strategic plan and objectives on use of personnel, budget and other resources

— Determine the core expertise of your team. What do you do best?

— Plan learning that supports by indentifying the competencies necessary to meet performance goals

— Focus on learning that addresses areas of weakness

— Support the transfer of learning into performance and results

How do I ensure this process is a success?

Make an annual learning plan

What are the benefits of an annual learning plan?

— With an annual learning plan, you can:
- Make a connection to the school's strategic objectives upfront
- Target training areas of greatest need and biggest payoff
- Find the best and most cost-effective way to get training

How to Get Results Activity

The best way to get results is to have a well-trained staff. Here are the basic steps for you to develop a training plan for your school:

1. Define learning needs linked to strategic plan
    - Identify your personal contribution to your school's mission, goals and objectives
    - Check into the use of new technology and new ways to use it
2. Validate your list of needs
    - Ensure that all the needs are learning needs
    - Figure out how the learning will contribute to overall solutions
    - Rank and prioritize in order of importance to the strategic plan
3. Determine the best strategies
    - Consider formal learning options
        - Coaching vs. conference
        - On-site vs. off-site
        - Customized vs. off-the-shelf
        - Expert vs. in-house instructor
4. Estimate cost
    - Include contracts, travel, per diem, special equipment
    - Weigh projected cost for different strategies and sources
5. Set priorities
    - Select the critical areas that need the most attention
    - Identify potential payoffs
    - Determine funding level and when you must draw the line
6. Determine how to evaluate results
    - Identify the measurable outcomes you expect to have
    - Make the link between outcome and strategic plan
    - Find a simple way to track progress

7. Share your plan with the entire staff
    - Generate understanding and promote "buy-in" of the plan
    - Lead by example: Demonstrate your commitment to learning for results
8. Execute and monitor
    - Assign responsibilities to implement the plan
    - Collect evaluation data
        — Track staff contributions
        — Document success stories
        — Make adjustments to plan as necessary

Read the section on results in the book and answer the following questions:

1. What are results?

___

2. What are the 4 reasons to conduct evaluations?

___

3. What actions are required when looking at results/evaluations?

___

Use this feedback spiral to continue the process

CONTINUOUS GROWTH THROUGH FEEDBACK SPIRALS

- REVISIT CLARIFY GOALS & PURPOSES
- PLAN
- TAKE ACTION/ EXPERIMENT
- ASSESS/GATHER EVIDENCE
- STUDY REFLECT EVALUATE
- MODIFY ACTIONS BASED ON NEW KNOWLEDGE

Adapted from Bena Kallick

Other Resources –
The Principal as Curriculum Leader Presentation

What does research say about shaping what is taught and tested?

" Principals can best discharge their leadership role if they develop a deep and broad knowledge base with respect to curriculum." –Glatthorn (2000)

What should the Principal do about State Standards?

- The practical response is to help teachers infuse standards in their instructional plans and delivery as part of their professional work.

What are the four curriculum levels?

- State Functions
- District Functions
- School Functions
- Classroom Functions

What are the school functions that principals should focus on?

- Develop the school's vision of a quality curriculum
- Build on the district vision
- Supplement the district's educational goals
- Develop its own program of studies
- Develop a learning-centered schedule
- Determine nature and extent of curriculum integration
- Align the curriculum
- Monitor and assist in the implementation of the curriculum
- Monitor and evaluate the curriculum

What are the classroom functions that principals should focus on?

- Unwrap the state standards by grade level
- Develop the 4-quarter plan
- Develop units of study using diary mapping (Lesson Plans)
- Deliver effective instructional strategies
- Enrich the curriculum and remediate learning
- Monitor and evaluate the curriculum

What is Total Instructional Alignment?

- Alignment versus teaching the test
    — Test questions change from year to year and within the same year with multiple versions
    — Tested concepts remain constant
    — Therefore: Teaching to the tested concepts will be our goal in Curriculum Mapping
- Alignment of the system
    — Horizontal (across grade levels)
    — Vertical (grade before and grade after)
- Alignment of standards, curriculum and assessments
    — Aligned to existing standards
    — Understanding exactly
        – What students are supposed to learn
        – How it will be assessed
- Alignment of instructional practices in the classroom
    — Understand and deliver instruction in a manner that includes
        – Standards
        – Curriculum
        – Assessments in their daily lessons

How we will plan for this initiative
- Determine who will be included
  - Principal
  - Curriculum Leadership Team (CLT)
  - Grade Level Teams (GLT)

Determine what the timeline will be
For example:
- July
  - Attend national mapping conference
  - Hold curriculum leadership team work sessions
  - Identify power standards in Reading/Math/Science
  - Prepare/present curriculum mapping model to staff
- August and continuing throughout the year
  - Use power standards in technology management systems
  - Design lessons using diary mapping format
  - Continue importing curriculum maps into technology management systems
  - Continue unwrapping standards
  - Develop 4-quarter plans using power standards

Determine how we will monitor the process
- Feedback spiral (continuous)
- Formative assessments
  - formal and informal
- Data analysis sessions
- Progress monitoring by collaborative teams
- Technology management systems
- Classroom walk-throughs
- Summative assessments

What Curriculum Data do we collect?

- Essential questions
- Content
- Skills
- Assessments
- Lessons
- Alignment to standards
- Information

What do we do with what we collect?

— Search for patterns

— Develop descriptive statistics

— Create Informational reports from mapping software

— Assessment

How do we use what we collect?

Integrate results from:

— Classroom assessments

— State standardized tests

– To build a professional community

What are some recommendations to building a professional community?

— Make data-driven decisions

— Have conversations between teachers designed to analyze:

— Cause-and-effect relationships

— Generate hypotheses

— Repeat the spiral feedback process

What are the key relationships I should build?

— School professional-parent relationships

— Teacher-principal relationships

— Teacher-teacher relationships

— Teacher-student relationships

"Relational trust in schools is directly correlated with higher student achievement"

—Anthony S. Bryk and Barbara Schneider

Other Resources —
How to Analyze Data - Implications for Instructional Planning and School-wide Reading Improvement Presentation

What is the data analysis process?

Objective 1

To create a streamlined process to analyze class data reports

Objective 2

To use the data to identify the students who are at risk for reading skill deficiencies and establish flexible skills groupings for direct instruction

What is the step-by-step process to analyzing data? (Response to Intervention RtI)

1. Determine primary indicators
2. Calculate class percentages
   - Benchmark
   - Strategic
   - Intensive
3. Indentify student weaknesses
   - Administer informal assessment
   - Analyze student errors
   - Use assessment reports to probe student details
   - Determine whole class needs
   - Determine individual student's targeted skill gaps
   - Determine common deficiencies among the class
4. Formulate a strategic plan by creating a watch list, move-up list and maintain list

5. Plan for Informal diagnostic testing
   - Choose appropriate informal assessements that:
     — Focus on one skill at a time
     — Are quick and efficient
6. Create instructional plans
   - Use data to create instructional plans for each student
   - Create targeted intervention groupings
   - Create flexible groupings for intervention
   - Students may start in one group, but as they progress (at their own pace) to fluency in a given skill, they may move into another group
7. Prepare your classroom lessons
   - Determine the first skill to be addressed
   - Prepare materials
   - Plan for centers and transitions
   - Develop classroom management and subroutines
8. Complete intervention logs
   - Track student progress through small groups
   - Track the activities used
   - Track the duration of lessons
   - Track Student performances
   - Progress monitor (Palm Pilots)
     — Intensive students = Every 2 weeks
     — Strategic students = Every 3 weeks
     — Cut-line benchmarks = Once a month

Other Resources — How to Align Your Total Programs

1. Implement onsite, school-specific, ongoing staff development
2. Review and select research-based literacy programs
3. Institute a 90-minute reading block (K-5) and a 45-minute reading block (6-8)
4. Purchase textbooks and materials for ALL core subject areas
5. Purchase new furniture for ALL offices and classrooms
6. Purchase additional computers and smart boards for all classrooms
7. Revise all school policies and procedures
8. Implement the Lovelady School Leadership Protocol
9. Implement a data-driven, student-focused instructional program in a collaborative culture
10. Deliver reading instruction and interventions designed to meet the indentified needs of all students at all abilities and skill levels
11. Begin student-focused coaching
12. Complete the set-up of the teacher center and the professional growth resource library for ongoing training, collaboration
13. Initiate "The Principal As Curriculum Leader: Shaping What Is Taught and Tested" goal
14. Develop the school's vision of what a quality curriculum contains
15. Develop learner-centered schedules
16. Determine the nature and extent of curriculum integration (horizontal and vertical)
17. Align the curriculum
18. Identify and unwrap power standards
19. Develop 4-quarter plans and identify and develop formative assessments at all grade levels
20. Align tutoring program using classroom instructional assessments and maps

21. Enrich the curriculum with additional hands-on activities to remediate learning
22. Monitor and evaluate the curriculum
23. Implement the AIMSWEB or similar assessment as a screener for Reading
24. Implement NWEA or similar testing assessment to measure standards-based instruction within the classroom.
25. Offer after-school tutoring to students in the "Approaches" category two weeks before testing.
26. Have teachers demonstrate all the following attributes to ensure student engagement throughout the learning process:
    — Direct students to be engaged in the academic learning
    — Direct all of the students to participate in the academic learning at the same time
    — Make student engagement mandatory by ensuring that all students are engaged throughout the academic learning process
27. Use the following feedback strategies with teachers
    — Reflective coaching
    — In and out coaching
    — On the Spot coaching
    — Side by Side coaching
    — Model coaching
    — Collaborative coaching
    — Grade level or department coaching
    — Team coaching
    — Model specific strategies
    — Plan and deliver lessons together (regular teacher/ESS teacher team teaching)
    — Whisper coaching

28. Use the Lovelady School Leadership Instructional Protocol Activity Sheets
    — Targeted Small Group Intervention Log
    — Effective Instructional Technology: Walk Through Form
    — Walk Through Observation Form
    — Effective Lesson Delivery Observation Notes
    — Four Types of Instruction Checklist
    — Reading Centers/ Small Group Instruction Form

Other Resources—
Aligning Instruction and Observation Activity Sheets

Lovelady School Leadership Instructional Protocol

Effective Instructional Techniques: Walk Through Form

Teacher _____
Grade _____
Date _____
Time _____
Observer _____

	Demonstrated Skills	1: Benchmark 2: Strategic 3: Intensive	Observer Feedback Notes
Preparation	Lesson plans with standards		
	Posts assignments/performance objectives posted		
	Organizes classroom and assignments		
	Makes materials easily accessible		
	Explicitly states objectives during the lesson		
Methods	Selects strategies/activities appropriate for objectives		
	Delivers instruction that is related to student's prior knowledge		
	Models and demonstrates effectively		
	Checks for understanding and makes adjustments		
	Provides students specific and immediate feedback		
	Encourages critical thinking		
	Displays the key vocabulary from lesson		
	Reviews, defines and/or demonstrates the key vocabulary used within the lesson		
Student Engagement	Directs students to be engaged in academic learning		
	Makes student engagement for all students mandatory throughout the academic learning		
	Provides alternative learning experiences		
	Provides meaningful individual/group practice		

Lovelady School Leadership Consulting © 2011 Reproducible

Effective Lesson Delivery Observation Notes

Teacher: _____ School Room #: _____ Grade/Content: _____

Date: _____ Start Time: _____ End Time: _____ # of Students: _____

Standard Posted: Y/N

Objective Posted: Y/N

Record what the teacher is doing and saying	Record corresponding student behaviors
Declarative Knowledge (those factors or ideas that we want students to know).	
Procedural Knowledge (processes or skills that we want students to know how to do).	
Anticipatory Set (how the teacher motivated the students to want to learn).	
Instruction (Declarative) **1. Constructing meaning** How did the teacher do this? ☐ 3-minute pause ☐ Learner uses all senses ☐ K-W-L ☐ Reciprocal teacher ☐ Other	

Lovelady School Leadership Consulting © 2011 Reproducible

Effective Lesson Delivery Observation Notes (con't next page)

Effective Lesson Delivery Observation Notes (con't)

2. Organizing knowledge How did the teacher help students assemble knowledge? ☐ Outline ☐ Build physical models ☐ Pictographs ☐ Used graphic organizers ☐ Other	
3. Storing the knowledge How did the teacher help student "lock" the information? ☐ Used symbols ☐ Rote memorization ☐ Mnemonics	
<u>**Instruction**</u> (Procedural) **1. Constructing Models** How did the teacher show students how to do something? ☐ Teacher demonstrated steps in process ☐ Teacher breaks down all steps	
2. Shaping How did the teacher adapt to different learning styles? ☐ Demonstrated and provided practice in varied ways ☐ Had students perform skills	
3. Internalizing How did the teacher provide sufficient practice for student mastery? ☐ Pair Share ☐ Triad Share ☐ White Board Demonstration ☐ Other engagement strategies	
Comments:	

Lovelady School Leadership Consulting © 2011 Reproducible

Walkthrough Observation Form

Teacher: _____ School Room #: _____ Grade/Content: _____

Date: _____ Start Time: _____ End Time: _____

Grouping Format: _____ Number in Group: _____ Group Performance Level: _____

In the box next to each General Feature indicate +, -, or NA. Check the box next to each observed area.

Instructor models instructional tasks when appropriate.	Instructor encourages student effort.
☐ Demonstrates the task (e.g., uses think-alouds) ☐ Proceeds in step-by-step fashion ☐ Limits language to demonstration of skill ☐ Makes eye contact with students, speaks clearly while modeling skill	☐ Provides feedback during and after task completion ☐ Provides specific feedback about student's accuracy and/or effort ☐ Majority of feedback is positive ☐ Celebrates or displays examples of student success in reading
Instructor provides explicit instruction.	**Students are engaged in the lesson during teacher-led instruction.**
☐ Sets the purpose for the instruction ☐ Identifies the important details of the concepts being taught ☐ Provides instructions that have only one interpretation ☐ Makes connection to previously learned material	☐ Gains student attention before initiating instruction ☐ Paces lesson to maintain attention ☐ Maintains close proximity to students ☐ Transitions quickly between tasks ☐ Intervenes with off-task students to maintain their focus
Instructor engages students in meaningful interactions with language during lesson.	**Students are engaged in the lesson during independent work.**
☐ Provides and elicits background information ☐ Emphasizes distinctive features of new concepts ☐ Uses visuals and manipulatives to teach content as necessary ☐ Makes relationships among concepts overt ☐ Engages students in discourse around new concepts ☐ Elaborates on students' responses	☐ Independent work routines and procedures have been previously taught ☐ Models task before allowing students to work independently ☐ Checks for student understanding of the task(s) ☐ Students use previously-learned strategies or routines when they come to a task they don't understand ☐ Independent work is completed with high level of accuracy
Instructor provides multiple opportunities for students to practice instructional tasks.	**Students are successfully completing activities at a high level of performance.**
☐ Provides more than one opportunity to practice each new skill ☐ Provides opportunities for practice after each step of instructions ☐ Elicits group responses when feasible ☐ Provides extra practice based on accuracy of student responses	☐ Elicits a high percentage of accurate responses from group ☐ Elicits a high percentage of accurate responses from individuals ☐ Holds same standard of accuracy for high performers and low performers
Instructor provides corrective feedback after initial student responses.	
☐ Provides affirmations for correct responses ☐ Promptly corrects errors with provision of correct model ☐ Limits corrective feedback language to the task at hand ☐ Ensures mastery of all students before moving on	
Comments:	

Four Types of Instruction Checklist

Teacher: _____ School Room #: _____ Grade/Content: _____

Date: _____ Start Time: _____ End Time: _____

Observer: _____

SYSTEMATIC ☐ Moves from simple → complex ☐ Known information → new information ☐ Skills are recursive ☐ Teacher demonstrates knowledge of skill sequences	**TEACHER ATTRIBUTES** ☐ Content posted in room ☐ Learning Centers ☐ Assessment (information diagnostics, instructional plans, progress monitoring) ☐ Writing samples/portfolio ☐ Lesson delivery moves from isolated to skill related to text ☐ Lesson plans ☐ Word wall (simple → complex) ☐ Use of instructional materials
EXPLICIT ☐ Appropriate modeling ☐ Guided practice ☐ Independent practice ☐ Provides effective corrective feedback ☐ Provides scaffolding	☐ Access prior knowledge ☐ State lesson objective ☐ Specific positive reinforcement ☐ Relate new info to known info ☐ Repeated opportunities for practice ☐ Checks for understanding and adapts as needed ☐ Student restates lesson objective

DIFFERENTIATED
☐ Whole Group
 	
☐ Small Group
☐ Uses assessment to determine instruction
☐ Scaled activities
☐ Cross-curricular
☐ Organized environment
	☐ Documentation that each student or group of students has had level opportunities/instruction is evident
	☐ Different modalities are evident in the different level activities
	☐ Time differentiation is evident
	☐ Additional groupings are evident
	☐ Differentiated presentations
	    o Chorus readings
	    o Thematic
	    o Puppets
	    o Collages
	☐ Examples of scaling up literacy circles and centers are evident within the classroom
	☐ Techniques for improving comprehension in grades K-8 for students who are weak in identified areas are evident

Adapted from SBSL (2008), Lovelady School Leadership Consulting © 2011 Reproducible

Four Types of Instruction Checklist (con't)

	☐ Evidence of student centers, literacy circles, bulletin boards that are interactive, movement of students throughout the room during lesson ☐ Differences in written work are posted to show writing process ☐ Differentiated questioning strategies and feedback are provided ☐ Evidence of different resources and monitoring data reflect student performance/progress in using these materials ☐ Materials are appropriate ☐ Differentiated questions are used ☐ Small group area set-up is evident ☐ Adaptations on graphic organizers are used ☐ Lesson plan indications are evident ☐ Furniture set-up accommodates effective teaching ☐ Alternate assessment methods are evident ☐ Flexible grouping is used ☐ Several levels of an objective are indicated In lesson plans Different types of graphic organizers are used to meet student needs

MULTI-SENSORY
    ☐ Uses manipulative objects when appropriate
    ☐ See, Hear, Say, Touch, Do activities are evident
    ☐ Classroom management accommodates individual student needs
    ☐ Maximizes instructional time
    ☐ Effective transitions are evident
    ☐ Classroom jobs are assigned to reflect cooperative learning
    ☐ Daily schedule to include Whole/Small/Individual groupings
    ☐ Routines and Subroutines well-established	

Adapted from SBSL (2008), Lovelady School Leadership Consulting © 2011 Reproducible

Reading Centers/Small Group Instruction Feedback Form

Teacher: _____ Grade Level: _____ Date: _____

Area of Observation	Yes	No	Not Observed	Comments:
Small Group Differentiated Instruction				
Centers start on time.				
Intervention Log reflects Center organization and grouping.				
Teacher instruction at "Teacher Center" is systematic, explicit and multisensory.				
Small-group instruction is provided at different levels depending on student need.				
A well-defined behavior management system is in place to guide student movement.				
At independent centers, students are working on activities that directly build reading skills.				
Centers are clearly defined and labeled.				
Students remain academically engaged during centers and independent work, and the use of manipulates are present during activities.				
If available, Aides are assigned a specific and clearly defined role during intervention time.				
Five Areas of Reading Addressed				
Phonemic Awareness:				
Activities are oral and include rhyming and manipulation of words, syllables, and sounds.				
Phonics:				
Language games and word play are used to connect sounds, letters and language.				
Fluency:				
Students are engaged at all times, sharing reading activities and keep individual logs of progress.				
Vocabulary:				
Vocabulary instruction is purposeful and ongoing as evidenced by lists of vocabulary words around the room.				
Comprehension:				
Teacher models and encourages students to use comprehension strategies throughout instruction and shared reading (summarizing, predicting, visualizing, semantic and graphic organizers, asking questions, monitoring and clarifying.)				
Comments:				

Lovelady School Leadership Consulting © 2011 Reproducible

Targeted Small Group Intervention Log

Students:_____ Month:_____

Grade:_____ Classroom Teacher:_____ Interventionist:_____

Targeted Intervention Focus (from Instructional Planning):

Week of:_____ Time:_____	Week of:_____ Time:_____
M T W Th F (Circle) Activity: _____ Materials:_____ Comments: Follow Up: Students Absent:	M T W Th F (Circle) Activity: _____ Materials:_____ Comments: Follow Up: Students Absent:
Week of:_____ Time:_____	Week of:_____ Time:_____
M T W Th F (Circle) Activity: _____ Materials:_____ Comments: Follow Up: Students Absent:	M T W Th F (Circle) Activity: _____ Materials:_____ Comments: Follow Up: Students Absent:

Lovelady School Leadership Consulting © 2011 Reproducible

REFERENCES

Alaska Statewide Mentor Project. Accessed at http://www.eed.State.ak.us/State_Board/pdf/Alaska_Statewide_Mentoring.Project.pdf on July 28, 2011.

Bamburg, J. & Andrews, R. (1990). School goals, principals and achievement. *School Effectiveness and School Improvement,* 2 (3), 175-191.

Bennis, W. (2003). *On Becoming a Leader.* Cambridge, Mass.: Perseus 3.

Bigelow, B. (1938). Building an effective training program for field salesmen. *Personnel, 14,* 142-150.

Block, P. (2003). *The Answer to How Is Yes: Acting on What Matters.* San Francisco: Berrett-Koehler.

Bossert, S.T., Dwyer, D.C., Rowan, B., & Lee, G.V. (1982). "The instructional management role of the principal." *Educational Administration Quarterly,* 18 (3), 34-64.

Boyd, V. (1992). School context: Bridge or barrier for change. Austin: Southwest Educational Development Laboratory.

Bradley, N., MacGregor, B., Buckley, M., Ryan-McNee, S., & McCoubrey, S. (May 2006). "Coaching Educational Leaders." *BC Educational Leadership Research.*

Brookover, et al. (1979). *School Social Systems and Student achievement schools can make a difference.* New York: Praeger.

Brookover, W.B., & Lezotte, L.W. (1979). *Changes in school characteristics coincident with changes in student achievement.* East Lansing, MI: The Institute for Research on Teaching.

Brookover, W. (1978). "Elementary school social climate and school achievement." *AmericanEducational Research Journal,* 15, 301-318.

Bush, R. N. (1984). "Effective Staff Development." San Francisco: Far West.

Clark, Donald, *Teamwork Survey,* 2004. Accessed at http:// www.nwlink.com/-donclark/leader/teamsuv.html on July 28, 2011.

Cohen, E., & Miller, R. (1980). "Coordination and control of instruction in schools." *Pacific Sociological Review,* 4, 446-473.

Collins, J. (2001). *Good to Great: Why Some Companies Make the Leap and Others Don't.* New York: HarperCollins Publishers Inc.

Covey, S.R. (1989). *The 7 Habits of Highly Effective People: Powerful Lessons in Personal Change.* New York: Simon & Schuster.

Covey, S.R. (1992). *Principle-centered Leadership.* New York: Simon & Schuster.

Department of Education and Early Childhood Development, Victoria, British Columbia. . Accessed at http://www.education.vic.gov.au/proflearning/bastowinstitute/leadership/procoach.htm on July 28, 2011.

Deming's Management Training. Accessed: June 28, 2006.

Diaz-Maggiolo, G. (2004). "A passion for learning: Teacher-centered professional development." Alexandria, VA: Association for Supervision and Curriculum Development.

Drake Beam Morin Inc (DBM) and the Human Capital Institute (HCI), *Trends in Executive Coaching*, 2008. Accessed at http://www.dbmgulf.com/pdf/Executive on July 28, 2011.

Duke, D. (1982). "Leadership functions and instructional effectiveness." *NASSP Bulletin*, 66, 5-9.

Duke, D. & Canady, L. (1991). *School Policy*. New York: McGraw Hill.

Eberts, R., & Stone J. (1988). "Student achievement in public schools: Do principals make a difference?" *Economics of Education Review*, 7, 291-299.

Elmore, R.F. (2000). *Building a New Structure for School Leadership*. New York: Albert Shanker Institute.

Fullan, M. (2009). "Have Theory, Will Travel" *Change Wars*. Bloomington, IN: Solution Tree.

Gershman, L. (1967). The effects of specific factors of the supervisor-subordinate coaching climate upon improvement of attitude and performance of the subordinate. *Dissertation Abstracts International*, 28 (5-B), 2122.

Glasman, N., & Binianimov, I. (1981). "Input-output analyses of schools." *Review of Educational Research*, 51, 509-539.

Glatthorn, A., (2000). *The Principal as Curriculum Leader: Shaping What is Taught and Tested*. Corwin Press, Thousand Oaks, CA.

Gorby, C. B. (1937). "Everyone gets a share of the profits." *Factory Management & Maintenance*, 95, 82-83.

Grady, C., et al. (2002). "The effects of encoding task on age-related differences in the functional neuroanatomy of face memory." Psychology and Aging 17 (1), 7-23, online publication date: 1-Jan-2002.

Griffith, J. (2000). "School climate as group evaluation and group consensus: Student and parent perceptions of the elementary school environment." *Elementary School Journal*, 101, 35–61.

Hall, G. E. & Hord, S. M. (1987). *Change in Schools: Facilitating the Process*. Albany, NY: State University of New York Press.

Hargreaves, A., & Fullan, M. (2009). *Change Wars*. Bloomington. IN: Solution Tree.

Hord, S.M. (1992). *Facilitative Leadership: The Imperative for Change*. Austin, TX: Southwest Educational Development Laboratory.

Hord, S.M., Rutherford, W.L., Huling-Austin, L., & Hall, G.E. (1987). *Taking Charge of Change*. Alexandria, VA. Association for Supervision and Curriculum Development.

Hoy, W. K., & Woolfolk, Hoy, A. (2006). *Instructional Leadership: A research-based guide to learning in schools* (2nd ed.). Boston: Allyn & Bacon/Longman.

Insights2Improvement, Inc. Professional Development Program Management. Accessed at http:/www.insights2improvement.com/Education Schools.html on July 28, 2011.

Joint Management Body/AMCSS Secretariat, *The Workload of Principals in Voluntary Secondary Schools* – A JMB Report 2005 , p. 15 – 22.

Joyce, B. & Showers, B. (1980). "Improving In-service Training: The Messages of Research." *Educational Leadership, 37(35), 379-385*.

Joyce, B., & Showers, B. (1987). *Student Achievement through Staff Development*. New York: Longman, Inc.

Joyce, B., & Showers, B. (1995). *Student Achievement through Staff Development*. (2nd ed.) White Plains, NY: Longman, Inc.

Joyce, B., & Showers, B. (2002). *Student Achievement through Staff Development*. (3rd ed.) Alexandria, VA: Association for Supervision and Curriculum Development.

Kallick, B. O., and Costa, A. L. (1995). *Assessment in the Learning Organization: Shifting the Paradigm*, (Chapter 13). Alexandra, VA: Association for Supervision and Curriculum Development,

Kentucky Department of Education. The Kentucky Cohesive Leadership System (KyCLS). Accessed at http://www.education.ky.gov/kde/administrative+resources/school+improvement/leadership+and+evaluation/kentucky+cohesive+leadership+system+(kycls)/leadership+performance+beginning+principal+coaching.htm on July 28, 2011.

Knowles, M.S. (1970, 1980) *The Modern Practice of Adult Education: Andragogy versus Pedagogy*. Englewood Cliffs: Prentice Hall/Cambridge.

Lovelady-Dawson, F., "Women and minorities in the principalship: Career opportunities and problems." *NASSP Bulletin*, 64, (440), p18-28, Dec 1980.

Mahler, W. R. (1964). Improving coaching skills. *Personnel Administration,* 27 (1), 28-33.

Marzano, R.J.; McNulty, B.A.,Waters, T. (2005) *School Leadership that Works: From Research to Results*. Alexandra, VA: Association for Supervision and Curriculum Development.

McDill, E., Rigsby, L., & Meyers, E. (1969). "Educational climates of high schools: Their effects and sources." *American Journal of Sociology*, 74, 567-586.

Mendez-Morse, S. (1992). *Leadership Characteristics that Facilitate School Change*. Austin: Southwest Educational Development Laboratory.

MetrixGlobal: (2001). "Executive briefing: Case study on the return on investment of executive coaching." *The Manchester Review*. 6, (1). Accessed at http://www.cpcusociety.org on July 28, 2011.

Michigan State University. The Michigan Principals Fellowship and Coaches Institute. Accessed at http://michiganprincipalsfellowship.org/SIG/ on July 28, 2011.

Miller, S., & Sayre, K. (1986, April). "Case studies of affluent effective schools." Paper presented at the annual meeting of the American Educational Research Association. San Francisco.

Mold, H. P. (1951). Developing top leaders—executive training. *Proceedings of the Annual Industrial Relations Conference*, 47-53.

Murphy, J., & Hallinger, P. (1989). "Equity as access to learning: Curricular and instructional differences." *Journal of Curriculum Studies*, 21, 129-149.

NYC Leadership Academy. Accessed at http://www.nycleadershipacademy.org/Principal_Coaching_Support on July 28, 2011.

Oakes, J. (1989). "Detracking schools: Early lessons from the field." *The Kappan Magazine*, 73, 448-454.

O'Neil, J. & Corzemius, A. (2006). *The Power of SMART Goals: Using Goals to Improve Student Learning form Adolescence*. Bloomington, IN: Solution Tree Press.

Peterson, K.D. & Deal, T.E. (2002). *Shaping School Culture Field Book*. San Francisco: Jossey-Bass.

Peterson, K.D. & Deal, T.E. (1999). *Shaping School Culture: The Heart of School Leadership*. San Francisco: Jossey-Bass.

Petterle, J. (1993). *Schools Flunk—-Kids Don't*. Glendale, CA: Griffin Publishing.

Purkey, S.C. & Smith, M.S. (1983). "Effective schools: A review." *The Elementary School Journal*, 83 (4), 427-452.

Reeves, D. (2009). "Level-five networks: Making significant change in complex organizations." *Change Wars*. Bloomington, IN: Solution Tree.

Region 10 Education Service Center. Richardson, Texas. Accessed at http://www.region10.org/Administrators/PrincipalCoachingService.html on July 28, 2011.

Reiss, K. (2007). Leadership Coaching for Educators. Thousand Oaks, CA: Corwin Press.

Rutter, M., Maughan, B., Mortimore, P. Ouston, J., & Smith, A. (1986). *Fifteen Thousand Hours: Secondary Schools and Their Effects on Children.* Cambridge, MA: Harvard University Press.

Salazar, P. (2008). High-Impact Leadership for High-Impact Schools. Larchmont, NY: Eye on Education.

Seattle University College of Education. Leadership Coaching. Accessed at http://www.seattleu.edu/coe/edadmin/leadershipcoaching.aspx on July 28, 2011.

Stinglhamber, F., & Vandenberghe, C. (2003). "Organizations and supervisors as sources of support and targets of commitment: A longitudinal study." *Journal of Organizational Behavior*, 24, 251–270.

Tallerico, M. (2005). *Supporting and Sustaining Teachers' Professional Development.* Thousand Oaks, CA: Corwin Press.

Vandenberghe, R., Daniëls, K., Dierynck, R. and Joris, C. (2003). *Starting Principals in Primary Schools: An Investigation on the Professional Development of School Leaders.* Leuven University Press, Leuven.

Villani, C.J. (1996). *The interaction of leadership and climate in four suburban schools: Limits and possibilities.* Doctoral dissertation, Fordham University, New York. (UMI No. 9729612)

Zeus, P. & Skiffington, S. (2002). *The Coaching at Work Toolkit.* Sydney: McGraw-Hill.

MyCoach Interactive™

MyCoach Interactive™ is an online leadership coaching resource for school principals, school administrators and those aspiring to be. We provide you with online resources you need to reach your professional leadership goals. MyCoach Interactive™ Membership includes:

- Free access (limited time) to all school leadership and school transformation resources in our membership library, including
    — Access to instructional video library
    — "How To" presentations
    — Tools and Techniques – Activities and other resources to use with your entire school improvement team
- Monthly Newsletter

We offer proven leadership strategies designed to get results that transform schools.

JOIN NOW.

Activate your membership today.
Visit www.LoveladySchoolLeadership.com
and click JOIN NOW.
1-877-368-0004

Obtain a free leadership profile

www.LoveladySchoolLeadership.com

Assess your leadership skills and discover what your behaviors and characteristics say about your expertise.

Visit www.LoveladySchoolLeadership.com
and click FREE ASSESSMENT. When you register you will:

- Take a school leadership survey and compare your responses to your peers. Your results may help you identify areas you might want to explore for modification or improvement.

- Get your free self-assessment via email. You can then take and tabulate results on your own. It is designed to allow school principals (and those aspiring to be) to assess key leadership skills necessary for effective performance in today's educational landscape.

www.ingramcontent.com/pod-product-compliance
Lightning Source LLC
Chambersburg PA
CBHW081216230426
43666CB00015B/2755